The Essentials of Prayer

THE ESSENTIALS OF PRAYER

E. M. BOUNDS

New Edition

BAKER BOOK HOUSE
Grand Rapids, Michigan 49516

ISBN: 0-8010-1005-5

Second printing, March 1994

Printed in the Unites States of America

Scripture quotations are taken from the King James Version of the Bible.

Contents

Publisher's Preface

FOR almost a century Edward McKendree Bounds's books on prayer have been classic works, stimulating and inspiring Christians to become prayer warriors. A forceful writer and very deep thinker, Bounds spent the last seventeen years of his life reading, writing, and praying. He rose at 4 A.M. daily for many years, and was indefatigable in his study of the Bible.

As breathing is a physical reality to us, so prayer was a reality for Bounds. He took the command, "Pray without ceasing," almost as literally as animate nature takes the law of the reflex nervous system, which controls our breathing.

Because Bounds so very diligently practiced what he preached, he was able to capture the essence of prayer, and his works live on to call today's Christians to higher discipleship and an energetic prayer life.

Baker Book House is pleased to present this new edition of *The Essentials of Prayer,* which was originally published in 1925. All type has been reset, and archaic words have been modernized, but we have been careful not to dim the intense spirit and clear challenges of this godly man who lived to pray and write about prayer.

Introduction

EDWARD MCKENDREE BOUNDS was born in northeastern Missouri on August 15, 1835. His father was instrumental in organizing Shelby County, Missouri, and was an original landholder in the county seat, Shelbyville. Bounds attended the Shelbyville one-room school, where he quickly learned to read and write. Because his father served as county clerk, the Bounds home was used for court sessions. This likely motivated Edward to study law, and he passed the bar exam shortly before he turned nineteen. He practiced law until he was twenty-four and then, somewhat suddenly, felt and answered the call to preach. He ardently read Scripture, savored John Wesley's sermons, and began preaching in a small church in the nearby town of Monticello.

During this time the Missouri populace was torn by dissension over slavery and preservation of the Union. Because Bounds was pastor of a congregation in the recently formed Methodist Episcopal Church, South (resulting from the North-South polarity), he was arrested in 1861 by Union troops in Brunswick, Missouri, and charged as a Confederate sympathizer. He was held (with other noncombatants) in a Federal prison in St. Louis for a year and a half. He then was transferred to Memphis and released in a prisoner exchange between the Union and the Confederacy. Shortly afterward he was sworn in as a Confederate chaplain and served concurrently in the Third Missouri Volunteer Infantry Regiment and the Missouri Fifth Infantry (the units had combined after the fighting at Atlanta).

Bounds comforted and prayed with troops under General John Bell Hood just before one of the most severe encounters in the Civil War erupted in the Battle of Franklin (the last great charge mounted by the Confederates). After General Hood's second defeat at Nashville, Bounds was among Confederate prisoners who were released upon the taking of an oath of loyalty to the United States. He returned to the site of the battle to pastor the Franklin Methodist Episcopal Church, South.

Bounds later was assigned to a pastorate in Selma, Alabama. There he met Emma Elizabeth Barnett from Washington, Georgia. In 1874 Bounds was transferred to St. Louis; he and Emma married in 1876. From this union two daughters, Celeste and Corneille, and a son, Edward, were born. Emma died eight years after they were married. About two years after Emma's death, Bounds married her cousin, Harriet Elizabeth Barnett. To them were born three sons (Samuel, Charles, and Osborne) and three daughters (Elizabeth, Mary, and Emmie). Two children died within a year, Edward, at the age of six, and Charles, shortly after his first birthday.

While in St. Louis, Bounds accepted the position of associate editor of the *St. Louis Advocate*, a regional Methodist journal. After nineteen months in this position he moved to Nashville to become the associate editor of the *Christian Advocate*, the official weekly paper for the entire Methodist Episcopal Church, South, denomination.

In 1894 E. M. Bounds concluded his duties in Nashville. He and his family moved to Washington, Georgia, to live in the Barnett House. Here he spent the final nineteen years of his life engaged in intercessory prayer, writing, and itinerant revival ministry. He typically arose at four o'clock every morning to be alone with God in prayer, usually praying until seven o'clock. E. M. Bounds died in 1913 with only two of his books published, *Preacher and Prayer* and *The Resurrection*. Homer W. Hodge, with some help from another friend of Bounds, Claude L. Chilton, assumed the task of bringing to publication nine more books written by E. M. Bounds.

Claude Chilton captured the essence of the books on prayer by Bounds when he said:

> These books are unfailing wells for a
> lifetime of spiritual water-drawing.
> They are hidden treasures,
> wrought in the darkness of dawn
> and the heat of the noon
> on the anvil of experience,
> and beaten into wondrous form
> by the mighty stroke of the divine.
> They are living voices
> whereby he, being dead,
> yet speaketh!

1

Prayer Takes In the Whole Man

PRAYER has to do with the entire man. Prayer takes in man in his whole being, mind, soul and body. It takes the whole man to pray, and prayer affects the entire man in its gracious results. As the whole nature of man enters into prayer, so also all that belongs to man is the beneficiary of prayer. All of man receives benefits in prayer. The whole man must be given to God in praying. The largest results in praying come to him who gives himself, all of himself, all that belongs to himself, to God. This is the secret of full consecration, and this is a condition of successful praying, and the sort of praying which brings the largest fruits.

The men of olden times who wrought well in prayer, who brought the largest things to pass, who moved God to do great things, were those who were entirely given over to God in their praying. God wants, and must have, all that there is in man in answering his prayers. He must have wholehearted men through whom to work out his purposes and plans concerning men. God must have men in their entirety. No double-minded man need apply. No vacillating man can be used. No man with a divided allegiance to God, and the world and self, can do the praying that is needed.

Holiness is wholeness, and so God wants holy men, men whole-hearted and true, for his service and for the work of praying. "And the very God of peace sanctify you wholly; and I pray God your whole spirit and soul and body be preserved blameless unto the coming of our Lord Jesus Christ." These are the sort of men God wants for leaders of the hosts of Israel, and these are the kind out of which the praying class is formed. Man is a trinity in one, and yet man is neither a trinity nor a dual creature when he prays, but a unit. Man is one in all the essentials and acts and attitudes of piety. Soul, spirit and body are to unite in all things pertaining to life and godliness. The body, first of all, engages in prayer, since it assumes the praying attitude in prayer. Prostration of the body becomes us in praying as well as prostration of the soul. The attitude of the body counts much in prayer, although it is true that the heart may be haughty and lifted up, and the mind listless and wandering, and the praying a mere form, even while the knees are bent in prayer.

Daniel kneeled three times a day in prayer. Solomon kneeled in prayer at the dedication of the temple. Our Lord in Gethsemane prostrated himself in that memorable season of praying just before his betrayal. Where there is earnest and faithful praying the body always takes on the form most suited to the state of the soul at the time. The body, that far, joins the soul in praying.

The entire man must pray. The whole man, life, heart, temper, mind, are in it. Each and all join in the prayer exercise. Doubt, double-mindedness, division of the affections, are all foreign to the closet. Character and conduct, undefiled, made whiter than snow, are mighty potencies, and are the most seemly beauties for the closet hour, and for the struggles of prayer.

A loyal intellect must conspire and add the energy and fire of its undoubting and undivided faith to that kind of an hour, the hour of prayer. Necessarily the mind enters into the praying. First of all, it takes thought to pray. The intellect teaches us we ought to pray. By serious thinking beforehand the mind prepares itself for approaching a throne of grace. Thought goes before entrance into the closet and prepares the way for true praying. It considers what will be asked for in the closet hour. True praying does not leave to the inspiration of the hour what will be the requests of that hour. As praying is asking for something definite of God, so, beforehand, the thought arises—

"What shall I ask for at this hour?" All vain and evil and frivolous thoughts are eliminated, and the mind is given over entirely to God, thinking of him, of what is needed, and what has been received in the past. By every token, prayer, in taking hold of the entire man, does not leave out the mind. The very first step in prayer is a mental one. The disciples took that first step when they said unto Jesus at one time, "Lord, teach us to pray." We must be taught through the intellect, and just in so far as the intellect is given up to God in prayer, will we be able to learn well and readily the lesson of prayer.

Paul spreads the nature of prayer over the whole man. It must be so. It takes the whole man to embrace in its godlike sympathies the entire race of man—the sorrows, the sins and the death of Adam's fallen race. It takes the whole man to run parallel with God's high and sublime will in saving mankind. It takes the whole man to stand with our Lord Jesus Christ as the one mediator between God and sinful man. This is the doctrine Paul teaches in his prayer-directory in the second chapter of his first epistle to Timothy.

Nowhere does it appear so clearly that it requires the entire man in all departments of his being, to pray than in this teaching of Paul. It takes the whole man to pray till all the storms which agitate his soul are calmed to a great calm, till the stormy winds and waves cease as by a godlike spell. It takes the whole man to pray till cruel tyrants and unjust rulers are changed in their natures and lives, as well as in their governing qualities, or till they cease to rule. It requires the entire man in praying till high and proud and unspiritual ecclesiastics become gentle, lowly and religious, till godliness and gravity bear rule in church and in state, in home and in business, in public as well as in private life.

It is man's business to pray; and it takes manly men to do it. It is godly business to pray and it takes godly men to do it. And it is godly men who give themselves over entirely to prayer. Prayer is far-reaching in its influence and in its gracious effects. It is intense and profound business which deals with God and his plans and purposes, and it takes whole-hearted men to do it. No half-hearted, half-brained, half-spirited effort will do for this serious, all-important, heavenly business. The whole heart,

the whole brain, the whole spirit, must be in the matter of praying, which is so mightily to affect the characters and destinies
of men. The answer of Jesus to the scribe as to what was the
first and greatest commandment was as follows:

> The Lord our God is one Lord; And thou shalt love the Lord
> thy God with all thy heart, and with all thy soul, and with all thy
> mind, and with all thy strength (Mark 12:29–30).

In one word, the entire man without reservation must love
God. So it takes the same entire man to do the praying which
God requires of men. All the powers of man must be engaged
in it. God cannot tolerate a divided heart in the love he requires
of men, neither can he bear with a divided man in praying.

In the first verse of the one hundred and nineteenth Psalm
the psalmist teaches this very truth in these words:

> Blessed are they that keep his testimonies, and seek him with
> the whole heart.

It takes whole-hearted men to keep God's commandments
and it demands the same sort of men to seek God. These are
they who are counted "blessed." Upon these whole-hearted ones
God's approval rests.

Bringing the case closer home to himself the psalmist makes
this declaration as to his practice: "With my whole heart have I
sought thee; O let me not wander from thy commandments"
(Ps. 119:21).

And further on, giving us his prayer for a wise and understanding heart, he tells us his purposes concerning the keeping
of God's law:

> Give me understanding and I shall keep thy law; Yea, I shall
> observe it with my whole heart (Ps. 119:34).

Just as it requires a whole heart given to God to gladly and
fully obey God's commandments, so it takes a whole heart to do
effectual praying.

Because it requires the whole man to pray, praying is no easy task. Praying is far more than simply bending the knee and saying a few words by rote.

> Tis not enough to bend the knee,
> And words of prayer to say;
> The heart must with the lips agree,
> Or else we do not pray.

Praying is no light and trifling exercise. While children should be taught early to pray, praying is no child's task. Prayer draws upon the whole nature of man. Prayer engages all the powers of man's moral and spiritual nature. It is this which explains somewhat the praying of our Lord as described in Hebrews 5:7:

> Who in the days of his flesh, when he had offered up prayers and supplications, with strong crying and tears, unto him that was able to save him from death, and was heard in that he feared.

It takes only a moment's thought to see how such praying of our Lord drew mightily upon all the powers of his being, and called into exercise every part of his nature. This is the praying which brings the soul close to God and which brings God down to earth.

Body, soul, and spirit are taxed and brought under tribute to prayer. David Brainerd makes this record of his praying:

> God enabled me to agonize in prayer till I was wet with perspiration, though in the shade and in a cool place.

The Son of God in Gethsemane was in an agony of prayer, which engaged his whole being:

> And when he was at the place, he said unto them, Pray ye that ye enter not into temptation. And he was withdrawn from them about a stone's cast, and kneeled down and prayed, saying, Father, if thou be willing, remove this cup from me; nevertheless, not my will, but thine, be done. And there appeared an angel unto him from heaven, strengthening him. And being in

an agony, he prayed more earnestly: and his sweat was as it were great drops of blood falling down to the ground (Luke 22:40–44).

Here was praying which laid its hands on every part of our Lord's nature, which called forth all the powers of his soul, his mind and his body. This was praying which took in the entire man.

Paul was acquainted with this kind of praying. In writing to the Roman Christians, he urges them to pray with him after this fashion:

> Now I beseech you, brethren, for the Lord Jesus Christ's sake, and for the love of the Spirit, that ye strive together with me in your prayers to God for me (Rom. 15:30).

The words, "strive together with me," tells of Paul's praying, and how much he put into it. It is not a docile request, not a little thing, this sort of praying, this "striving with me." It is of the nature of a great battle, a conflict to win, a great battle to be fought. The praying Christian, as the soldier, fights a life-and-death struggle. His honor, his immortality, and eternal life are all in it. This is praying as the athlete struggles for the mastery, and for the crown, and as he wrestles or runs a race. Everything depends on the strength he puts in it. Energy, ardor, swiftness, every power of his nature is in it. Every power is quickened and strained to its very utmost. Littleness, half-heartedness, weakness and laziness are all absent.

Just as it takes the whole man to pray successfully, so in turn the whole man receives the benefits of such praying. As every part of man's complex being enters into true praying, so every part of that same nature receives blessings from God in answer to such praying. This kind of praying engages our undivided hearts, our full consent to be the Lord's, our whole desires.

God sees to it that when the whole man prays, in turn the whole man shall be blessed. His body takes in the good of praying, for much praying is done specifically for the body. Food and raiment, health and bodily vigor, come in answer to praying. Clear mental action, right thinking, an enlightened understanding, and safe reasoning powers, come from praying. Divine guidance means God so moving and impressing the mind, that we shall make wise and safe decisions. "The meek will he guide in judgment."

Many a praying preacher has been greatly helped just at this point. The unction of the Holy One which comes upon the preacher invigorates the mind, loosens up thought and gives utterance. This is the explanation of former days when men of very limited education had such wonderful liberty of the Spirit in praying and in preaching. Their thoughts flowed as a stream of water. Their entire intellectual machinery felt the impulse of the divine Spirit's gracious influences.

And, of course, the soul receives large benefits in this sort of praying. Thousands can testify to this statement. So we repeat, that as the entire man comes into play in true, earnest effectual praying, so the entire man, soul, mind and body, receives the benefits of prayer.

2

Prayer and Humility

To be humble is to have a low estimate of one's self. It is to be modest, lowly, with a disposition to seek obscurity. Humility retires itself from the public gaze. It does not seek publicity nor hunt for high places, neither does it care for prominence. Humility is retiring in its nature. Self-abasement belongs to humility. It is given to self-depreciation. It never exalts itself in the eyes of others nor even in the eyes of itself. Modesty is one of its most prominent characteristics.

In humility there is the total absence of pride, and it is at the very farthest distance from anything like self-conceit. There is no self-praise in humility, Rather it has the disposition to praise others. "In honor preferring one another." It is not given to self-exaltation. Humility does not love the uppermost seats and aspire to the high places. It is willing to take the lowliest seat and prefers those places where it will be unnoticed. The prayer of humility is after this fashion:

> Never let the world break in,
> Fix a mighty gulf between;
> Keep me humble and unknown,
> Prized and loved by God alone.

Humility does not have its eyes on self, but rather on God and others. It is poor in spirit, meek in behavior, lowly in heart.

19

"With all lowliness and meekness, with long-suffering, forbearing one another in love."

The parable of the Pharisee and publican is a sermon in brief on humility and self-praise. The Pharisee, given over to self-conceit, wrapped up in himself, seeing only his own self-righteous deeds, catalogues his virtues before God, despising the poor publican who stands afar off. He exalts himself, gives himself over to self-praise, is self-centered, and goes away unjustified, condemned and rejected by God.

The publican sees no good in himself, is overwhelmed with self-depreciation, far removed from anything which would take any credit for any good in himself, does not presume to lift his eyes to heaven, but with downcast countenance smites himself on his breast, and cries out, "God be merciful to me, a sinner."

Our Lord with great preciseness gives us the sequel of the story of these two men, one utterly devoid of humility, the other utterly submerged in the spirit of self-depreciation and lowliness of mind.

> I tell you this man went down to his house justified rather than the other; for every one that exalteth himself shall be abased; and he that humbleth himself shall be exalted (Luke 18:14).

God puts a great price on humility of heart. It is good to be clothed with humility as with a garment. It is written, "God resisteth the proud, but giveth grace to the humble." That which brings the praying soul near to God is humility of heart. That which gives wings to prayer is lowliness of mind. That which gives ready access to the throne of grace is self-depreciation. Pride, self-esteem, and self-praise effectually shut the door of prayer. He who would come to God must approach him with self hid from his own eyes. He must not be puffed-up with self-conceit, nor be possessed with an over-estimate of his virtues and good works.

Humility is a rare Christian grace, of great price in the courts of heaven, entering into and being an inseparable condition of effectual praying. It gives access to God when other qualities fail. It takes many descriptions to describe it, and many definitions to define it. It is a rare and retiring grace. Its full portrait is found only in the Lord Jesus Christ. Our prayers must be set low before they can ever rise high. Our prayers must have much of the dust on them before they can ever have much of the glory of the skies in them. In our Lord's teaching, humility has such prominence in his system of religion, and is such a distinguishing feature of his character, that to leave it out of his lesson on prayer would be very unseemly, would not comport with his character, and would not fit into his religious system.

The parable of the Pharisee and publican stands out in such bold relief that we must again refer to it. The Pharisee seemed to be inured to prayer. Certainly he should have known by that time how to pray, but alas! like many others, he seemed never to have learned this invaluable lesson. He leaves business and business hours and walks with steady and fixed steps up to the house of prayer. The position and place are well chosen by him. There is the sacred place, the sacred hour, and the sacred name, each and all invoked by this seemingly praying man. But this praying ecclesiastic, though schooled to prayer, by training and by habit, prays not. Words are uttered by him, but words are not prayer. God hears his words only to condemn him. A death-chill has come from those formal lips of prayer—a death-curse from God is on his words of prayer. A solution of pride has entirely poisoned the prayer offering of that hour. His entire praying has been impregnated with self-praise, self-congratulation, and self-exaltation. That season of temple going has had no worship whatever in it.

On the other hand, the publican, smitten with a deep sense of his sins and his inward sinfulness, realizing how poor in spirit he is, how utterly devoid of anything like righteousness, goodness, or any quality which would commend him to God, his pride within utterly blasted and dead, falls down with humiliation and despair before God, while he utters a sharp cry for mercy for his sins and his guilt. A sense of sin and a realization of utter unworthiness has fixed the roots of humility deep down in his soul, and has oppressed self and eye and heart, downward to the dust. This is the picture of humility against pride in praying. Here we see by sharp contrast the utter worthlessness of self-righteousness, self-exaltation, and self-praise in praying, and the great value, the beauty and the divine commendation which comes to humility of heart, self-depreciation, and self-condemnation when a soul comes before God in prayer.

Happy are they who have no righteousness of their own to plead and no goodness of their own of which to boast. Humility flourishes in the soil of a true and deep sense of our sinfulness and our nothingness. Nowhere does humility grow so rankly and so rapidly and shine so brilliantly, as when it feels all guilty, confesses all sin, and trusts all grace. "I the chief of sinners am, but Jesus died for me." That is praying ground, the ground of humility, low down, far away seemingly, but in reality brought nigh by the blood of the Lord Jesus Christ. God dwells in the lowly places. He makes such lowly places really the high places to the praying soul.

> Let the world their virtue boast,
> Their works of righteousness;
> I, a wretch undone and lost,
> Am freely saved by grace;
> Other title I disclaim,
> This, only this, is all my plea,
> I the chief of sinners am,
> But Jesus died for me.

Humility is an indispensable requisite of true prayer. It must be an attribute, a characteristic of prayer. Humility must be in the praying character as light is in the sun. Prayer has no beginning, no ending, no being, without humility. As a ship is made for the sea, so prayer is made for humility, and so humility is made for prayer.

Humility is not abstraction from self, nor does it ignore thought about self. It is a many-phased principle. Humility is born by looking at God, and his holiness, and then looking at self and man's unholiness. Humility loves obscurity and silence, dreads applause, esteems the virtues of others, excuses their faults with mildness, easily pardons injuries, fears contempt less and less, and sees baseness and falsehood in pride. A true nobleness and greatness are in humility. It knows and reveres the inestimable riches of the cross, and the humiliations of Jesus

Christ. It fears the luster of those virtues admired by men, and loves those that are more secret and which are prized by God. It draws comfort even from its own defects, through the abasement which they occasion. It prefers any degree of compunction before all light in the world.

Somewhat after this order of description is that definable grace of humility, so perfectly drawn in the publican's prayer, and so entirely absent from the prayer of the Pharisee. It takes many sittings to make a good picture of it.

Humility holds in its keeping the very life of prayer. Neither pride nor vanity can pray. Humility, though, is much more than the absence of vanity and pride. It is a positive quality, a substantial force, which energizes prayer. There is no power in prayer to ascend without it. Humility springs from a lowly estimate of ourselves and of our deservings. The Pharisee prayed not, though well schooled and accustomed to pray, because there was no humility in his praying. The publican prayed, though banned by the public and receiving no encouragement from church sentiment, because he prayed in humility. To be clothed with humility is to be clothed with a praying garment. Humility is just feeling little because we *are* little. Humility is realizing our unworthiness because we *are* unworthy, the feeling and declaring ourselves sinners because we *are* sinners. Kneeling well becomes us as the attitude of prayer, because it betokens humility.

The Pharisee's proud estimate of himself and his supreme contempt for his neighbor closed the gates of prayer to him, while humility opened wide those gates to the defamed and reviled publican.

That fearful saying of our Lord about the works of big, religious workers in the latter part of the Sermon on the Mount, is called out by proud estimates of work and wrong estimates of prayer:

> Many will say to me in that day, Lord, Lord, have we not prophesied in thy name? and in thy name have cast out devils? and in thy name done many wonderful works? And then will I profess unto them, I never knew you: depart from me, ye that work iniquity (Matt. 7:22–23).

Humility is the first and last attribute of Christlike religion, and the first and last attribute of Christlike praying. There is no Christ without humility. There is no praying without humility. If you would learn well the art of praying, then learn well the lesson of humility.

How graceful and imperative does the attitude of humility become to us! Humility is one of the unchanging and exacting attitudes of prayer. Dust, ashes, earth upon the head, sackcloth for the body, and fasting for the appetites were the symbols of humility for the Old Testament saints. Sackcloth, fasting, and ashes brought Daniel a lowliness before God, and brought Gabriel to him. The angels are fond of the sackcloth-and-ashes men.

How lowly the attitude of Abraham, the friend of God, when pleading for God to stay his wrath against Sodom! "Which am but sackcloth and ashes." With what humility does Solomon appear before God! His grandeur is abased, and his glow and majesty are retired as he assumes the rightful attitude before God: "I am but a little child, and know not how to go out or to come in."

The pride of doing sends its poison all through our praying. The same pride of being infects our prayers, no matter how well-worded they may be. It was this lack of humility, this self-applauding, this self-exaltation, which kept the most religious man of Christ's day from being accepted of God. And the same thing will keep us in this day from being accepted of him.

> O that now I might decrease!
> O that all I am might cease!
> Let me into nothing fall!
> Let my Lord be all in all.

3

Prayer and Devotion

DEVOTION has a religious signification. The root of devotion is to devote to a sacred use. So that devotion in its true sense has to do with religious worship. It stands intimately connected with true prayer. Devotion is the particular frame of mind found in one entirely devoted to God. It is the spirit of reverence, of awe, of godly fear. It is a state of heart which appears before God in prayer and worship. It is foreign to everything like lightness of spirit, and is opposed to levity and noise and bluster. Devotion dwells in the realm of quietness and is still before God. It is serious, thoughtful, meditative.

Devotion belongs to the inner life and lives in the closet, but also appears in the public services of the sanctuary. It is a part of the very spirit of true worship, and is of the nature of the spirit of prayer.

Devotion belongs to the devout man, whose thoughts and feelings are devoted to God. Such a man has a mind given up wholly to religion, and possesses a strong affection for God and an ardent love for his house. Cornelius was "a devout man, one that feared God with all his house, which gave much alms to the people, and prayed always." "Devout men carried Stephen to his burial." "One Ananias, a devout man, according to the law," was sent unto Saul when he was blind, to tell him what the Lord would have him do. God can wonderfully use such men, for devout men are his chosen agents in carrying forward his plans.

25

Prayer promotes the spirit of devotion, while devotion is favorable to the best praying. Devotion furthers prayer and helps to drive prayer home to the object which it seeks. Prayer thrives in the atmosphere of true devotion. It is easy to pray when in the spirit of devotion. The attitude of mind and the state of heart implied in devotion make prayer effectual in reaching the throne of grace. God dwells where the spirit of devotion resides. All the graces of the Spirit are nourished and grow well in the environment created by devotion. Indeed, these graces grow nowhere else but here. The absence of a devotional spirit means death to the graces born in a renewed heart. True worship finds congeniality in the atmosphere made by a spirit of devotion. While prayer is helpful to devotion, at the same time devotion reacts on prayer, and helps us to pray.

Devotion engages the heart in prayer. It is not an easy task for the lips to try to pray while the heart is absent from it. The charge which God at one time made against his ancient Israel was, that they honored him with their lips while their hearts were far from him.

The very essence of prayer is the spirit of devotion. Without devotion prayer is an empty form, a vain round of words. Sad to say, much of this kind of prayer prevails, today, in the church. This is a busy age, bustling and active, and this bustling spirit has invaded the church of God. Its religious performances are many. The church works at religion with the order, precision and force of real machinery. But too often it works with the heartlessness of the machine. There is much of the treadmill movement in our ceaseless round and routine of religious doings. We pray without praying. We sing without singing with the Spirit and the understanding. We have music without the praise of God being in it, or near it. We go to church by habit, and come home all too gladly when the benediction is pronounced. We read our accustomed chapter in the Bible, and feel quite relieved when the task is done. We say our prayers by rote, as a schoolboy recites his lesson, and are not sorry when the Amen is uttered.

Religion has to do with everything but our hearts. It engages our hands and feet, it takes hold of our voices, it lays its hands on our money, it affects even the postures of our bodies, but it does not take hold of our affections, our desires, our zeal, and make us serious, desperately in earnest, and cause us to be quiet and worshipful in the presence of God. Social affinities attract us to the house of God, not the spirit of the occasion. Church membership keeps us after a fashion decent in outward conduct and with some shadow of loyalty to our baptismal vows, but the heart is not in the thing. It remains cold, formal, and unimpressed amid all this outward performance, while we give ourselves over to self-congratulation that we are doing wonderfully well religiously.

Why all these sad defects in our piety? Why this modern perversion of the true nature of the religion of Jesus Christ? Why is the modern type of religion so much like a jewel-case with the precious jewels gone? Why so much of this handling religion with the hands, often not too clean or unsoiled, and so little of it felt in the heart and witnessed in the life?

The great lack of modern religion is the spirit of devotion. We hear sermons in the same spirit with which we listen to a lecture or hear a speech. We visit the house of God just as if it were a common place, on a level with the theater, the lecture-room or the forum. We look upon the minister of God not as the divinely-called man of God, but merely as a sort of public speaker, on a plane with the politician, the lawyer, or the average speech maker, or the lecturer. Oh, how the spirit of true and genuine devotion would radically change all this for the better! We handle sacred things just as if they were the things of the world. Even the sacrament of the Lord's Supper becomes a mere religious performance, no preparation for it beforehand, and no meditation and prayer afterward. Even the sacrament of Baptism has lost much of its solemnity, and degenerated into a mere form, with nothing specially in it.

We need the spirit of devotion, not only to salt our secularities, but to make praying real prayers. We need to put the spirit of devotion into Monday's business as well as in Sunday's worship. We need the spirit of devotion, to recollect always the presence of God, to be always doing the will of God, to direct all things always to the glory of God.

The spirit of devotion puts God in all things. It puts God not merely in our praying and church-going, but in all the concerns of life. "Whether, therefore, ye eat or drink, or whatsoever ye do, do all to the glory of God." The spirit of devotion makes the common things of earth sacred, and the little things great. With this spirit of devotion, we go to business on Monday directed by the very same influence, and inspired by the same influences by which we went to church on Sunday. The spirit of devotion makes a Sabbath out of Saturday, and transforms the shop and the office into a temple of God.

The spirit of devotion removes religion from being a thin veneer, and puts it into the very life and being of our souls. With it religion ceases to be doing a mere work, and becomes a heart, sending its rich blood through every artery and beating with the pulsations of vigorous and radiant life.

The spirit of devotion is not merely the aroma of religion, but the stalk and stem on which religion grows. It is the salt which penetrates and makes savory all religious acts. It is the sugar which sweetens duty, self-denial and sacrifice. It is the bright coloring which relieves the dullness of religious performances. It dispels frivolity and drives away all skin-deep forms of worship, and makes worship a serious and deep-seated service, impregnating body, soul and spirit with its heavenly infusion. Let us ask in all seriousness, has this highest angel of heaven, this heavenly spirit of devotion, this brightest and best angel of earth, left us? When the angel of devotion has gone, the angel of prayer has lost its wings, and it becomes a deformed and loveless thing.

The ardor of devotion is in prayer. In the fourth chapter of Revelation, verse eight, we read: "And they rest not day nor night, saying, Holy, Holy, Holy, Lord God Almighty, which was, and is, and is to come." The inspiration and center of their rapturous devotion is the holiness of God. That holiness of God claims their attention, inflames their devotion. There is nothing cold, nothing dull, nothing wearisome about them or their heavenly worship. "They rest not day nor night." What zeal! What unfainting ardor and ceaseless rapture! The ministry of prayer, if it be anything worthy of the name, is a ministry of ardor, a ministry of unwearied and intense longing after God and after his holiness.

The spirit of devotion pervades the saints in heaven and characterizes the worship of heaven's angelic intelligences. No devotionless creatures are in that heavenly world. God is there, and his very presence begets the spirit of reverence, of awe, and of real fear. If we would be partakers with them after death, we must first learn the spirit of devotion on earth before we get there.

These living creatures in their restless, tireless attitude after God, and their rapt devotion to his holiness, are the perfect symbols and manifestations of true prayer and its ardor. Prayer must be aflame. Its ardor must consume. Prayer without fervor is as a sun without light or heat, or as a flower without beauty or fragrance. A soul devoted to God is a fervent soul, and prayer is the creature of that flame. He only can truly pray who is all aglow for holiness, for God, and for heaven.

Activity is not strength. Work is not zeal. Moving about is not devotion. Activity often is the unrecognized symptom of spiritual weakness. It may be hurtful to piety when made the substitute for real devotion in worship, The colt is much more active than its mother, but she is the wheel-horse of the team, pulling the load without noise or bluster or show. The child is more active than the father, who may be bearing the rule and burdens of an empire on his heart and shoulders. Enthusiasm is more active than faith, though it cannot remove mountains nor call into action any of the omnipotent forces which faith can command.

A feeble, lively, showy religious activity may spring from many causes. There is much running around, much stirring about, much going here and there, in present-day church life, but sad to say, the spirit of genuine, heartfelt devotion is strangely lacking. If there be real spiritual life, a deep-toned activity will spring from it. But it is an activity springing from strength and not from weakness. It is an activity which has deep roots, many and strong.

In the nature of things, religion must show much of its growth above ground. Much will be seen and be evident to the eye. The flower and fruit of a holy life, abounding in good works, must be seen. It cannot be otherwise. But the surface growth must be based on a vigorous growth of unseen life and hidden roots. Deep down in the renewed nature must the roots of religion go which is seen on the outside. The external must have a deep internal groundwork. There must be much of the invisible and the underground growth, or else the life will be feeble and short-lived, and the external growth sickly and fruitless.

In the Book of Isaiah these words are written:

> They that wait upon the Lord shall renew their strength; they shall mount up with wings as eagles; they shall run, and not be weary; and they shall walk, and not faint (40:31).

This is the genesis of the whole matter of activity and strength of the most energetic, exhaustless and untiring nature. All this is the result of waiting on God.

There may be much of activity induced by drill, created by enthusiasm, the product of the weakness of the flesh, the inspiration of volatile, short-lived forces. Activity is often at the expense of more solid, useful elements, and generally to the total neglect of prayer. To be too busy with God's work to commune with God, to be busy with doing church work without taking time to talk to God about his work, is the highway to backsliding, and many people have walked therein to the hurt of their immortal souls.

Notwithstanding great activity, great enthusiasm, and much hurrah for the work, the work and the activity will be but blindness without the cultivation and the maturity of the graces of prayer.

4

Prayer, Praise, and Thanksgiving

PRAYER, praise, and thanksgiving all go in company. A close relationship exists between them. Praise and thanksgiving are so near alike that it is not easy to distinguish between them or define them separately. The Scriptures join these three things together. Many are the causes for thanksgiving and praise. The Psalms are filled with many songs of praise and hymns of thanksgiving, all pointing back to the results of prayer. Thanksgiving includes gratitude. In fact thanksgiving is but the expression of an inward conscious gratitude to God for mercies received. Gratitude is an inward emotion of the soul, involuntarily arising therein, while thanksgiving is the voluntary expression of gratitude.

Thanksgiving is oral, positive, active. It is the giving out of something to God. Thanksgiving comes out into the open. Gratitude is secret, silent, negative, passive, not showing its being till expressed in praise and thanksgiving. Gratitude is felt in the heart. Thanksgiving is the expression of that inward feeling.

Thanksgiving is just what the word itself signifies—the giving of thanks to God. It is giving something to God in words which we feel at heart for blessings received. Gratitude arises from a contemplation of the goodness of God. It is bred by serious meditation on what God has done for us. Both gratitude and thanksgiving point to, and have to do with God and his

31

mercies. The heart is consciously grateful to God. The soul gives expression to that heartfelt gratitude to God in words or acts.

Gratitude is born of meditation on God's grace and mercy. "The Lord hath done great things for us, whereof we are glad." Herein we see the value of serious meditation. "My meditation of him shall be sweet." Praise is begotten by gratitude and a conscious obligation to God for mercies given. As we think of mercies past, the heart is inwardly moved to gratitude.

> I love to think on mercies past,
> And future good implore;
> And all my cares and sorrows cast
> On him whom I adore.

Love is the child of gratitude. Love grows as gratitude is felt, and then breaks out into praise and thanksgiving to God: "I love the Lord because he hath heard my voice and my supplication." Answered prayers cause gratitude, and gratitude brings forth a love that declares it will not cease praying: "Because he hath inclined his ear unto me, therefore will I call upon him as long as I live." Gratitude and love move to larger and increased praying.

Paul appeals to the Romans to dedicate themselves wholly to God, a living sacrifice, and the constraining motive is the mercies of God:

> I beseech you, therefore, brethren, by the mercies of God, that ye present your bodies a living sacrifice, holy, acceptable unto God, which is your reasonable service (Rom. 12:1).

Consideration of God's mercies not only begets gratitude, but also induces a large consecration to God of all we have and are. So that prayer, giving, and consecration are all linked together inseparably.

Gratitude and thanksgiving always looks back at the past though it may also take in the present. But prayer always looks to the future. Thanksgiving deals with things already received. Prayer deals with things desired, asked for, and expected. Prayer turns to gratitude and praise when the things asked for have been granted by God.

As prayer brings things to us which beget gratitude and thanksgiving, so praise and gratitude promote prayer, and induce more praying and better praying.

Gratitude and thanksgiving forever stand opposed to all murmurings at God's dealings with us, and all complainings at our lot. Gratitude and murmuring never abide in the same heart at the same time. An unappreciative spirit has no standing beside gratitude and praise. And true prayer corrects complaining and promotes gratitude and thanksgiving. Dissatisfaction at one's lot, and a disposition to be discontented with things which come to us in the providence of God, are foes to gratitude and enemies to thanksgiving.

The murmurers are ungrateful people. Appreciative men and women have neither the time nor disposition to stop and complain. The bane of the wilderness journey of the Israelites on their way to Canaan was their proneness to murmur and complain against God and Moses. For this, God was several times greatly grieved, and it took the strong praying of Moses to avert God's wrath because of these murmurings. The absence of gratitude left no room nor disposition for praise and thanksgiving, just as it is so always. But when these same Israelites were brought through the Red Sea dry shod, while their enemies were destroyed, there was a song of praise led by Miriam, the sister of Moses. One of the leading sins of these Israelites was forgetfulness of God and his mercies, and ingratitude of soul. This brought forth murmurings and lack of praise, as it always does.

When Paul wrote to the Colossians to let the word of Christ dwell in their hearts richly and to let the peace of God rule therein, he said to them, "and be ye thankful," and adds, "admonishing yourselves in psalms and hymns and spiritual songs, singing with grace in your hearts unto the Lord."

Further on, in writing to these same Christians, he joins prayer and thanksgiving together: "Continue in prayer, and watch in the same with thanksgiving."

And writing to the Thessalonians, he again joins them in union: "Rejoice evermore. Pray without ceasing. In everything give thanks, for this is the will of God concerning you."

> We thank thee, Lord of heaven and earth,
> Who hast preserved us from our birth;
> Redeemed us oft from death and dread,
> And with thy gifts our table spread.

Wherever there is true prayer, there thanksgiving and gratitude stand hard by, ready to respond to the answer when it comes. For as prayer brings the answer, so the answer brings forth gratitude and praise. As prayer sets God to work, so answered prayer sets thanksgiving to work. Thanksgiving follows answered prayer just as day succeeds night.

True prayer and gratitude lead to full consecration, and consecration leads to more praying and better praying. A consecrated life is both a prayer life and a thanksgiving life.

The spirit of praise was once the boast of the primitive church. This spirit abode on the tabernacles of these early Christians, as a cloud of glory out of which God shined and spoke. It filled their temples with the perfume of costly, flaming incense. That this spirit of praise is sadly deficient in our present-day congregations must be evident to every careful observer. That it is a mighty force in projecting the gospel, and its body of vital forces, must be equally evident. To restore the spirit of praise to our congregations should be one of the main points with every true pastor. The normal state of the church is set forth in the declaration made to God in Psalm 65: "Praise waiteth for thee, O Lord, and unto thee shall the vow be performed."

Praise is so distinctly and definitely wedded to prayer, so inseparably joined, that they cannot be divorced. Praise is dependent on prayer for its full volume and its sweetest melody.

Singing is one method of praise, not the highest it is true, but it is the ordinary and usual form. The singing service in our churches has much to do with praise, for according to the character of the singing will be the genuineness or the measure of praise. The singing may be so directed as to have in it elements which deprave and debauch prayer. It may be so directed as to drive away everything like thanksgiving and praise. Much of modern singing in our churches is entirely foreign to anything like hearty, sincere praise to God.

The spirit of prayer and of true praise go hand in hand. Both are often entirely dissipated by the flippant, thoughtless, light singing in our congregations. Much of the singing lacks serious thought and is devoid of everything like a devotional spirit. Its lustiness and sparkle may not only dissipate all the essential features of worship, but may substitute the flesh for the spirit.

Giving thanks is the very life of prayer. It is its fragrance and music, its poetry and its crown. Prayer bringing the desired answer breaks out into praise and thanksgiving. So that whatever interferes with and injures the spirit of prayer necessarily hurts and dissipates the spirit of praise.

The heart must have in it the grace of prayer to sing the praise of God. Spiritual singing is not to be done by musical taste or talent, but by the grace of God in the heart. Nothing helps praise so mightily as a gracious revival of true religion in the church. The conscious presence of God inspires song. The angels and the glorified ones in heaven do not need artistic directors to lead them, nor do they care for paid choirs to chime in with their heavenly doxologies of praise and worship. They are not dependent on singing schools to teach them the notes and scale of singing. Their singing involuntarily breaks forth from the heart.

God is immediately present in the heavenly assemblies of the angels and the spirits of just men made perfect. His glorious presence creates the song, teaches the singing, and impregnates their notes of praise. It is so on earth. God's presence begets singing and thanksgiving, while the absence of God from our congregations is the death of song, or, which amounts to the same, makes the singing lifeless, cold, and formal. His conscious presence in our churches would bring back the days of praise and would restore the full chorus of song.

Where grace abounds, song abounds. When God is in the heart, heaven is present and melody is there, and the lips overflow out of the abundance of the heart. This is as true in the private life of the believer as it is so in the congregations of the saints. The decay of singing, the dying down and out of the spirit of praise in song, means the decline of grace in the heart and the absence of God's presence from the people.

The main design of all singing is for God's ear and to attract his attention and to please him. It is "to the Lord," for his glory, and to his honor. Certainly it is not for the glorification of the paid choir, to exalt the wonderful musical powers of the singers, nor is it to draw the people to the church, but it is for the glory of God and the good of the souls of the congregation. Alas! How far has the singing of choirs of churches of modern times departed from this idea! It is no surprise that there is no life, no power, no unction, no spirit, in much of the church singing heard in this day. It is sacrilege for any but sanctified hearts and holy lips to direct the singing part of the service of God's house of prayer. Much of the singing in churches would do credit to the opera house, and might satisfy as mere entertainments, pleasing the ear, but as a part of real worship, having in it the spirit of praise and prayer, it is a fraud, an imposition on spiritually minded people, and entirely unacceptable to God. The cry should go out afresh, "Let all the people praise the Lord," for "it is good to sing praises unto our God; for it is pleasant; and praise is comely."

The music of praise, for there is real music of soul in praise, is too hopeful and happy to be denied. All these are in the "giving of thanks." In Philippians, prayer is called "requests." "Let your requests be made known unto God," which describes prayer as an asking for a gift, giving prominence to the thing asked for, making it emphatic, something to be given by God and received by us, and not something to be done by us. And all this is closely connected with gratitude to God, "with thanksgiving, let your requests be made known unto God."

God does much for us in answer to prayer, but we need from him many gifts, and for them we are to make special prayer. According to our special needs, so must our praying be. We are to be special and particular and bring to the knowledge of God by prayer, supplication and thanksgiving, our particular requests, the things we need, the things we greatly desire. And with it all, accompanying all these requests, there must be thanksgiving.

It is indeed a pleasing thought that what we are called upon to do on earth, to praise and give thanks, the angels in heaven and the redeemed disembodied spirits of the saints are doing also. It is still further pleasing to contemplate the glorious hope that what God wants us to do on earth, we will be engaged in doing throughout an unending eternity. Praise and thanksgiving will be our blessed employment while we remain in heaven. Nor will we ever grow weary of this pleasing task.

Joseph Addison sets before us, in verse, this pleasing prospect:

> Through every period of my life
> Thy goodness I'll pursue;
> And after death, in distant worlds,
> The pleasing theme renew.
>
> Through all eternity to thee
> A grateful song I'll raise;
> But Oh! eternity's too short
> To utter all thy praise.

5

Prayer and Trouble

TROUBLE and prayer are closely related to other. Prayer is of great value to trouble. Trouble often drives men to God in prayer, while prayer is but the voice of men in trouble. There is great value in prayer in the time of trouble. Prayer often delivers out of trouble, and still oftener gives strength to bear trouble, ministers comfort in trouble, and begets patience in the midst of trouble. Wise is he in the day of trouble who knows his true source of strength and who fails not to pray.

Trouble belongs to the present state of man on earth. "Man that is born of a woman is of few days and full of trouble." Trouble is common to man. There is no exception in any age or clime or station. Rich and poor alike, the learned and the ignorant, one and all are partakers of this sad and painful inheritance of the fall of man. "There hath no temptation taken you but such as is common to man." The "day of trouble" dawns on every one at some time in his life. "The evil days come and the years draw nigh" when the heart feels its heavy pressure.

That is an entirely false view of life and shows supreme ignorance that expects nothing but sunshine and looks only for ease, pleasure, and flowers. It is this class who are so sadly disappointed and surprised when trouble breaks into their lives. These are the ones who know not God, who know nothing of his disciplinary dealings with his people and who are prayerless.

What an infinite variety there is in the troubles of life! How diversified the experiences of men in the school of trouble! No two people have the same troubles under like environments. God deals with no two of his children in the same way. And as God varies his treatment of his children, so trouble is varied. God does not repeat himself. He does not run in a rut. He has not one pattern for every child. Each trouble is proportioned to each child. Each one is dealt with according to his own peculiar case.

Trouble is God's servant, doing his will unless he is defeated in the execution of that will. Trouble is under the control of Almighty God, and is one of his most efficient agents in fulfilling his purposes and in perfecting his saints. God's hand is in every trouble which breaks into the lives of men. Not that he directly and arbitrarily orders every unpleasant experience of life. Not that he is personally responsible for every painful and afflicting thing which comes into the lives of his people. But no trouble is ever turned loose in this world and comes into the life of saint or sinner, but comes with divine permission, and is allowed to exist and do its painful work with God's hand in it or on it, carrying out his gracious designs of redemption.

All things are under divine control. Trouble is neither above God nor beyond his control. It is not something in life independent of God. No matter from what source it springs nor whence it arises, God is sufficiently wise and able to lay his hand upon it without assuming responsibility for its origin, and work it into his plans and purposes concerning the highest welfare of his saints. This is the explanation of that gracious statement in Romans, so often quoted, but the depth of whose meaning has rarely been sounded, "And we know that all things work together for good to them that love God."

Even the evils brought about by the forces of nature are his servants, carrying out his will and fulfilling his designs. God even claims the locusts, the earthworm, the caterpillar are his servants, "My great army," used by him to correct his people and discipline them.

Trouble belongs to the disciplinary part of the moral government of God. This is a life of probation, where the human race is on probation. It is a season of trial. Trouble is not penal in its nature. It belongs to what the Scriptures call "chastening." "Whom the Lord loveth he chasteneth, and scourgeth every son whom he receiveth." Speaking accurately, punishment does not belong to this life. Punishment for sin will take place in the next world. God's dealings with people in this world are of the nature of discipline. They are corrective processes in his plans concerning man. It is because of this that prayer comes in when trouble arises. Prayer belongs to the discipline of life.

As trouble is not sinful in itself, neither is it the evidence of sin. Good and bad alike experience trouble. As the rain falls alike on the just and unjust, so drought likewise comes to the righteous and the wicked. Trouble is no evidence whatever of the divine displeasure. Scripture instances without number disprove any such idea. Job is a case in point, where God bore explicit testimony to his deep piety, and yet God permitted Satan to afflict him beyond any other man for wise and beneficent purposes. Trouble has no power in itself to interfere with the relations of a saint to God. "Who shall separate us from the love of Christ? Shall tribulation, or distress, or persecution, or famine, or nakedness, or peril, or sword ?"

Three words practically the same in the processes of divine discipline are found, temptation, trial, and trouble, and yet there is a difference between them. Temptation is really a solicitation to evil arising from the devil or born in the carnal nature of man. Trial is testing. It is that which proves us, tests us, and makes us stronger and better when we submit to the trial and work together with God in it. "My brethren, count it all joy when ye fall into temptations; knowing this, that the trying of your faith worketh patience."

Peter speaks along the same line:

> Wherein ye greatly rejoice, though now for a season, if need be, ye are in heaviness through manifold temptations; that the trial of your faith, being much more precious than of gold that perisheth, though it be tried with fire, might be found unto praise and honour and glory at the appearing of Jesus Christ (1 Peter 1:6–7).

The third word is trouble itself, which covers all the painful, sorrowing, and grievous events of life. And yet temptations and trials might really become troubles. So that all evil days in life might well be classed under the head of the "time of trouble." And such days of trouble are the lot of all men. Enough to know that trouble, no matter from what source it comes, becomes in God's hand his own agent to accomplish his gracious work concerning those who submit patiently to him, who recognize him in prayer, and who work together with God.

Let us settle down at once to the idea that trouble arises not by chance, and neither occurs by what men call accident. "Although affliction cometh not forth of the dust, neither doth trouble spring out of the ground, yet man is born unto trouble as the sparks fly upward." Trouble naturally belongs to God's moral government, and is one of his invaluable agents in governing the world.

When we realize this, we can the better understand much that is recorded in the Scriptures, and can have a clearer conception of God's dealings with his ancient Israel. In God's dealings with them, we find what is called a history of divine providence, and providence always embraces trouble. No one can understand the story of Joseph and his old father Jacob unless he takes into the account trouble and its varied offices. God takes account of trouble when he urges his prophet Isaiah on this wise:

> Comfort ye, comfort ye my people, saith your God. Speak ye comfortably to Jerusalem, and cry unto her, that her warfare is accomplished, that her iniquity is pardoned (Isa. 40:1–2).

There is a distinct note of comfort in the gospel for the praying saints of the Lord, and he is a wise scribe in divine things who knows how to minister this comfort to the broken-hearted and sad ones of earth. Jesus himself said to his sad disciples, "I will not leave you comfortless."

All the foregoing has been said that we may rightly appreciate the relationship of prayer to trouble. In the time of trouble, where does prayer come in? The psalmist tells us: "Call upon me in the day of trouble; I will deliver thee, and thou shalt glorify me." Prayer is the most appropriate thing for a soul to do in the "time of trouble." Prayer recognizes God in the day of trouble. "It is the Lord; let him do what seemeth him good." Prayer sees God's hand in trouble, and prays about it. Nothing more truly shows us our helplessness than when trouble comes. It brings the strong man low, it discloses our weakness, it brings a sense of helplessness. Blessed is he who knows how to turn to God in "the time of trouble." If trouble is of the Lord, then the most natural thing to do is to carry the trouble to the Lord, and seek grace and patience and submission. It is the time to inquire in the trouble, "Lord, what wilt thou have me to do?" How natural and reasonable for the soul, oppressed, broken, and bruised, to bow low at the footstool of mercy and seek the face of God. Where could a soul in trouble more likely find solace than in the closet?

Alas! trouble does not always drive men to God in prayer. Sad is the case of him who, when trouble bends his spirit down and grieves his heart, yet knows not whence the trouble comes nor knows how to pray about it. Blessed is the man who is driven by trouble to his knees in prayer!

> Trials must and will befall;
> But with humble faith to see
> Love inscribed upon them all—
> This is happiness to me.
>
> Trials make the promise sweet
> Trials give new life to prayer;
> Bring me to my Savior's feet
> Lay me low, and keep me there.

Prayer in the time of trouble brings comfort, help, hope, and blessings, which, while not removing the trouble, enable the saint the better to bear it and to submit to the will of God. Prayer opens the eyes to see God's hand in trouble. Prayer does not interpret God's providences, but it does justify them and recognize God in them. Prayer enables us to see wise ends in trouble. Prayer in trouble drives us away from unbelief, saves us from

doubt, and delivers from all vain and foolish questionings
because of our painful experiences. Let us not lose sight of the
tribute paid to Job when all his troubles came to the culminat-
ing point: "In all this Job sinned not, nor charged God foolishly."

Alas! for vain, ignorant men, without faith in God and knowing nothing of God's discip linary processes in dealing with
men, who charge God foolishly when troubles come, and who
are tempted to "curse God." How silly and vain are the complainings, the murmurings, and the rebellion of men in the time
of trouble! What need to read again the story of the children of
Israel in the wilderness! And how useless is all our fretting, our
worrying over trouble, as if such unhappy doings on our part
could change things! "And which of you with taking thought,
can add to his stature one cubit?" How much wiser, how much
better, how much easier to bear life's troubles when we take
everything to God in prayer.

Trouble has wise ends for the praying ones, and these find it
so. Happy is he who, like the psalmist, finds that his troubles
have been blessings in disguise. "It is good for me that I have
been afflicted, that I might learn thy statutes. I know, O Lord,
that thy judgments are right, and that thou in faithfulness hast
afflicted me."

> O who could bear life's stormy doom,
> Did not thy wing of love
> Come brightly wafting through the gloom
> Our peace branch from above.
>
> Then sorrow, touched by thee, grows bright,
> With more than rapture's ray;
> As darkness shows us worlds of light
> We never saw by day.

Of course, it may be conceded that some troubles are really
imaginary. They have no existence other than in the mind. Some
are anticipated troubles, which never arrive at our door. Others
are past troubles, and there is much folly in worrying over
them. Present troubles are the ones requiring attention and

demanding prayer. "Sufficient unto the day is the evil thereof." Some troubles are self-originated. We are their authors. Some of these originate involuntarily with us, some arise from our ignorance, some come from our carelessness. All this can be readily admitted without breaking the force of the statement that they are the subjects of prayer, and should drive us to prayer. What father casts off his child who cries to him when the little one from its own carelessness has stumbled and fallen and hurt itself? Does not the cry of the child attract the ears of the father even though the child be to blame for the accident? "Whatever things ye desire" takes in every event of life, even though we are responsible for some events.

Some troubles are human in their origin. They arise from second causes. They originate with others and we are the sufferers. This is a world where often the innocent suffer the consequences of the acts of others. This is a part of life's incidents. Who has not at some time suffered at the hands of others? But even these are allowed to come in the order of God's providence, are permitted to break into our lives for beneficent ends, and may be prayed over. Why should we not carry our hurts, our wrongs and our privations, caused by the acts of others, to God in prayer? Are such things outside of the realm of prayer? Are they exceptions to the rule of prayer? Not at all. And God can and will lay his hand upon all such events in answer to prayer, and cause them to work for us "a far more exceeding and eternal weight of glory."

Nearly all of Paul's troubles arose from wicked and unreasonable men. Read the story as he gives it in 2 Corinthians 11:23–33.

So also some troubles are directly of Satanic origin. Quite all of Job's troubles were the offspring of the devil's scheme to break down Job's integrity, to make him charge God foolishly and to curse God. But are these not to be recognized in prayer? Are they to be excluded from God's disciplinary processes? Job did not do so. Hear him in those familiar words. "The Lord gave, and the Lord hath taken away. Blessed be the name of the Lord."

O what a comfort to see God in all of life's events! What a relief to a broken, sorrowing heart to see God's hand in sorrow!

What a source of relief is prayer in unburdening the heart in grief!

> O thou who driest the mourner's tear,
> How dark this world would be,
> If, when deceived and wounded here,
> We could not fly to thee?
>
> The friends who in our sunshine live,
> When winter comes are flown,
> And he who has but tears to give,
> Must weep those tears alone.
>
> But thou wilt heal the broken heart,
> Which, like the plants that throw
> Their fragrance from the wounded part,
> Breathes sweetness out of woe.

But when we survey all the sources from which trouble comes, it all resolves itself into two invaluable truths: First, that our troubles at last are of the Lord. They come with his consent. He is in all of them, and is interested in us when they press and bruise us. And secondly, that our troubles, no matter what the cause, whether of ourselves, or men or devils, or even God himself, we are warranted in taking them to God in prayer, in praying over them, and in seeking to get the greatest spiritual benefits out of them.

Prayer in the time of trouble tends to bring the spirit into perfect subjection to the will of God, to cause the will to be conformed to God's will, and saves from all murmurings over our lot, and delivers from everything like a rebellious heart or a spirit critical of the Lord. Prayer sanctifies trouble to our highest good. Prayer so prepares the heart that it softens under the disciplining hand of God. Prayer places us where God can bring to us the greatest good, spiritual and eternal. Prayer allows God to freely work with us and in us in the day of trouble. Prayer removes everything in the way of trouble, bringing to us the sweetest, the highest and greatest good. Prayer permits God's servant, trouble, to accomplish its mission in us, with us and for us.

The end of trouble is always good in the mind of God. If trouble fails in its mission, it is either because of prayerlessness or unbelief, or both. Being in harmony with God in the dispensations of his providence, always makes trouble a blessing. The good or evil of trouble is always determined by the spirit in which it is received. Trouble proves a blessing or a curse, just according as it is received and treated by us. It either softens or hardens us. It either draws us to prayer and to God or it drives us from God and from the closet. Trouble hardened Pharaoh till finally it had no effect on him, only to make him more desperate and to drive him farther from God. The same sun softens the wax and hardens the clay. The same sun melts the ice and dries out the moisture from the earth.

As is the infinite variety of trouble, so also is there infinite variety in the relations of prayer to other things. How many are the things which are the subject of prayer! It has to do with everything which concerns us, with everybody with whom we have to do, and has to do with all times. But especially does prayer have to do with trouble. "This poor man cried and the Lord heard him, and saved him out of all his troubles." O the blessedness, the help, the comfort of prayer in the day of trouble! And how marvelous the promises of God to us in the time of trouble!

> Because he hath set his love upon me, therefore will I deliver him; I will set him on high because he hath known my name. He shall call upon me, and I will answer him; I will be with him in trouble; I will deliver him and honour him (Ps. 91:14–15).

> If pain afflict, or wrongs oppress,
> If cares distract, or fears dismay;
> If guilt deject, if sin distress,
> In every case, still watch and pray.

How rich in its sweetness, how far-reaching in the realm of trouble, and how cheering to faith, are the words of promise which God delivers to his believing, praying ones, by the mouth of Isaiah:

> But now, thus saith the Lord that created thee, O Jacob, and he that formed thee, O Israel, Fear not: for I have redeemed thee, I have called thee by thy name; thou art mine. When thou passest through the waters, I will be with thee; and through the rivers, they shall not overflow thee: when thou walkest through the fire, thou shalt not be burned; neither shall the flame kindle upon thee. For I am the Lord thy God, the Holy One of Israel, thy Savior (Isa. 43:1–3).

6

Prayer and Trouble
(*Continued*)

In the New Testament there are three words used which embrace trouble. These are tribulation, suffering, and affliction, words differing somewhat, and yet each of them practically meaning trouble of some kind. Our Lord put his disciples on notice that they might expect tribulation in this life, teaching them that tribulation belonged to this world, and they could not hope to escape it; that they would not be carried through this life on flowery beds of ease. How hard to learn this plain and patent lesson! "In the world ye shall have tribulation; but be of good cheer; I have overcome the world." There is the encouragement. As he had overcome the world and its tribulations, so might they do the same. Paul taught the same lesson throughout his ministry, when in confirming the souls of the brethren, and exhorting them to continue in the faith, he told them that "we must, through much tribulation, enter into the kingdom of God." He himself knew this by his own experience, for his pathway was anything but smooth and flowery.

He it is who uses the word "suffering" to describe the troubles of life, in that comforting passage in which he contrasts life's troubles with the final glory of heaven, which shall be the reward of all who patiently endure the ills of divine providence:

49

For I reckon that the sufferings of this present time are not
worthy to be compared with the glory which shall be revealed
in us (Rom. 8:18).

And he it is who speaks of the afflictions which come to the
people of God in this world, and regards them as light as compared with the weight of glory awaiting all who are submissive,
patient, and faithful in all their troubles:

For our light affliction, which is but for a moment, worketh
for us a far more exceeding and eternal weight of glory (2 Cor.
4:17).

But these present afflictions can work for us only as we co-
operate with God in prayer. As God works through prayer, it is
only through this means he can accomplish his highest ends for
us. His providence works with greatest effect with his praying
ones. These know the uses of trouble and its gracious designs.
The greatest value in trouble comes to those who bow lowest
before the throne.

Paul, in urging patience in tribulation, connects it directly with
prayer, as if prayer alone would place us where we could be
patient when tribulation comes. "Rejoicing in hope, patient in
tribulation, continuing instant in prayer." He here couples up
tribulation and prayer, showing their close relationship and the
worth of prayer in begetting and culturing patience in tribulation.
In fact there can be no patience exemplified when trouble comes,
only as it is secured through instant and continued prayer. In the
school of prayer is where patience is learned and practiced.

Prayer brings us into that state of grace where tribulation is
not only endured, but where there is under it a spirit of rejoicing. In showing the gracious benefits of justification, in Romans
5:3, Paul says:

And not only so, but we glory in tribulation also: knowing
that tribulation worketh patience; and patience, experience; and
experience, hope; and hope maketh not ashamed; because the
love of God is shed abroad in our hearts by the Holy Spirit
which is given unto us.

What a chain of graces are here set forth as flowing from tribulation! What successive steps to a high state of religious experience! And what rich fruits result from even painful tribulation!

To the same effect are the words of Peter in his first epistle, in his strong prayer for those Christians to whom he writes; thus showing that suffering and the highest state of grace are closely connected; and intimating that it is through suffering we are to be brought to those higher regions of Christian experience:

> But the God of all grace, who hath called us unto his eternal glory by Christ Jesus, after that ye have suffered a while, make you perfect, stablish, strengthen, settle you (1 Peter 5:10).

It is in the fires of suffering that God purifies his saints and brings them to the highest things. It is in the furnace their faith is tested, their patience is tried, and they are developed in all those rich virtues which make up Christian character. It is while they are passing through deep waters that he shows how close he can come to his praying, believing saints.

It takes faith of a high order and a Christian experience far above the average religion of this day, to count it joy when we are called to pass through tribulation. God's highest aim in dealing with his people is in developing Christian character. He is after begetting in us those rich virtues which belong to our Lord Jesus Christ. He is seeking to make us like himself. It is not so much work that he wants in us. It is not greatness. It is the presence in us of patience, meekness, submission to the divine will, prayerfulness which brings everything to him. He seeks to beget his own image in it. And trouble in some form tends to do this very thing, for this is the end and aim of trouble. This is its work. This is the task it is called to perform. It is not a chance incident in life, but has a design in view, just as it has an all-wise designer back of it, who makes trouble his agent to bring forth the largest results.

The writer of the Epistle to the Hebrews gives us a perfect directory of trouble, comprehensive, clear, and worthwhile to be studied. Here is "chastisement," another word for trouble, coming from a Father's hand, showing God is in all the sad and afflictive events of life. Here is its nature and its gracious design. It is not punishment in the accurate meaning of that word, but the means God employs to correct and discipline his children in dealing with them on earth. Then we have the fact of the evidence of being his people, namely, the presence of chastisement. The ultimate end is "that we may be partakers of his holiness," which is but another way of saying that all this disciplinary process is to the end that God may make us like himself. What an encouragement, too, that, chastisement is no evidence of anger or displeasure on God's part, but is the strong proof of his love. Let us read the entire directory on this important subject:

> And ye have forgotten the exhortation which speaketh unto you as unto children, My son, despise not thou the chastening of the Lord, nor faint when thou art rebuked of him: For whom the Lord loveth he chasteneth, and scourgeth every son whom he receiveth. If ye endure chastening, God dealeth with you as with sons; for what son is he whom the father chasteneth not? But if ye be without chastisement, whereof all are partakers, then are ye bastards, and not sons.
>
> Furthermore we have had fathers of our flesh which corrected us, and we gave them reverence: shall we not much rather be in subjection unto the Father of spirits, and live? For they verily for a few days chastened us after their own pleasure; but he for our profit, that we might be partakers of his holiness. Now no chastening for the present seemeth to be joyous, but grievous; nevertheless afterward it yieldeth the peaceable fruit of righteousness unto them which are exercised thereby (Heb. 12:6–11).

Just as prayer is wide in its range, taking in everything, so trouble is infinitely varied in its uses and designs. It takes trouble sometimes to arrest attention, to stop men in the busy rush of life, and to awaken them to a sense of their helplessness and their need and sinfulness. Not till King Manasseh was bound with thorns and carried away into a foreign land and got into deep trouble, was he awakened and brought back to God. It was then he humbled himself and began to call upon God.

The Prodigal was independent and self-sufficient when in prosperity, but when money and friends departed, and he began to be in want, then it was he "came to himself," and decided to return to his father's house, with prayer and confession on his lips. Many a man who has forgotten God has been arrested, caused to consider his ways, and brought to remember God and pray by trouble. Blessed is trouble when it accomplishes this in men!

It is for this among other reasons that Job says:

> Behold, happy is the man whom God correcteth: therefore, despise not thou the chastening of the Almighty: For he maketh sore, and bindeth up; he woundeth, and his hands make whole. He shall deliver thee in six troubles: yea, in seven there shall no evil touch thee (Job 5:17–19).

One thing more might be named. Trouble makes earth undesirable and causes heaven to loom up large in the horizon of hope. There is a world where trouble never comes. But the path of tribulation leads to that world. Those who are there went there through tribulation. What a world set before our longing eyes which appeals to our hopes, as sorrows like a cyclone sweep over us! Hear John, as he talks about it and those who are there:

> What are these which are arrayed in white robes? and whence came they? . . . And he said to me, These are they which came out of great tribulation, and have washed their robes, and made them white in the blood of the Lamb. . . . And God shall wipe away all tears from their eyes (Rev. 7:13–14, 17).

> There I shall bathe my weary soul,
> In seas of heavenly rest,
> And not a wave of trouble roll,
> Across my peaceful breast.

Oh, children of God, you who have suffered, who have been sorely tried, whose sad experiences have often brought broken spirits and bleeding hearts, cheer up! God is in all your troubles, and he will see that all shall "work together for good," if you will but be patient, submissive, and prayerful.

7

Prayer and God's Work

GOD has a great work on hand in this world. This work is involved in the plan of salvation. It embraces redemption and providence. God is governing this world, with its intelligent beings, for his own glory and for their good. What, then, is God's work in this world? Rather what is the end he seeks in his great work? It is nothing short of holiness of heart and life in the children of fallen Adam. Man is a fallen creature, born with an evil nature, with an evil bent, unholy propensities, sinful desires, wicked inclinations. Man is unholy by nature, born so. "They go astray as soon as they be born, speaking lies." God's entire plan is to take hold of fallen man and to seek to change him and make him holy. God's work is to make holy men out of unholy men. This is the very end of Christ coming into the world:

For this purpose the Son of God was manifested that he might destroy the works of the devil (1 John 3:8).

God is holy in nature and in all his ways, and he wants to make man like himself.

As he which hath called you is holy, so be ye holy in all manner of conversation; because it is written, Be ye holy, for I am holy (1 Peter 1:15–16).

This is being Christlike. This is following Jesus Christ. This is the aim of all Christian effort. This is the earnest, heartfelt desire of every truly regenerated soul. This is what is to be constantly and earnestly prayed for. It is that we may be made holy. Not that we must make ourselves holy, but we must be cleansed from all sin by the precious atoning blood of Christ, and be made holy by the direct agency of the Holy Spirit. Not that we are to *do* holy, but rather to *be* holy. Being must precede doing. First be, then do. First, obtain a holy heart, then live a holy life. And for this high and gracious end God has made the most ample provisions in the atoning work of our Lord and through the agency of the Holy Spirit.

The work of God in the world is the implantation, the growth and the perfection of holiness in his people. Keep this ever in mind. But we might ask just now, Is this work advancing in the church? Are men and women being made holy? Is the present-day church engaged in the business of making holy men and women? This is not a vain and speculative question. It is practical, pertinent, and all important.

The present-day church has vast machinery. Her activities are great, and her material prosperity is unparalleled. The name of religion is widespread and well-known. Much money comes into the Lord's treasury and is paid out. But here is the question: Does the work of holiness keep pace with all this? Is the burden of the prayers of church people to be made holy? Are our preachers really holy men? Or to go back a little further, are they hungering and thirsting after righteousness, desiring the sincere milk of the Word that they may grow thereby? Are they really seeking to be holy men? Of course men of intelligence are greatly needed in the pulpit, but prior to that, and primary to it, is the fact that we need holy men to stand before dying men and proclaim the salvation of God to them.

Ministers, like laymen, and no more so than laymen, must be holy men in life, in conversation and in temper. They must be examples to the flock of God in all things. By their lives they are to preach as well as to speak. Men in the pulpit are needed who are spotless in life, circumspect in behavior, "without rebuke and blameless in the midst of a crooked and perverse nation, among whom they are to shine in the world." Are our preachers of this type of men? We are simply asking the question. Let the reader make up his own judgment. Is the work of holiness making progress among our preachers?

Again let us ask: Are our leading laymen examples of holiness? Are they seeking holiness of heart and life? Are they praying men, ever praying that God would fashion them according to his pattern of holiness? Are their business ways without stain of sin, and their gains free from the taint of wrongdoing? Have they the foundation of solid honesty, and does uprightness bring them into elevation and influence? Does business integrity and probity run parallel with religious activity, and with churchly observance?

Then, while we are pursuing our investigation, seeking light as to whether the work of God among his people is making progress, let us ask further as to our women. Are the leading women of our churches dead to the fashions of this world, separated from the world, not conformed to the world's maxims and customs? Are they in behavior as becometh holiness, teaching the young women by word and life the lessons of soberness, obedience, and home-keeping? Are our women noted for their praying habits? Are they patterns of prayer?

How searching are all these questions? And will anyone dare say they are impertinent and out of place? If God's work be to make men and women holy, and he has made ample provisions in the law of prayer of doing this very thing, why should it be thought impertinent and useless to propound such personal and pointed questions as these? They have to do directly with the work and with its progress and its perfection. They go to the very seat of the disease. They hit the spot.

We might as well face the situation first as last. There is no use to shut our eyes to real facts. If the church does not do this sort of work—if the church does not advance its members in holiness of heart and life—then all our show of activities and all our display of church work are a delusion and a snare.

But let us ask as to another large and important class of people in our churches. They are the hope of the future church. To them all eyes are turned. Are our young men and women growing in sobermindedness and reverence, and in all those graces which have their root in the renewed heart, which mark solid and permanent advance in the divine life? If we are not growing in holiness, then we are doing nothing religious nor abiding.

Material prosperity is not the infallible sign of spiritual prosperity. The former may exist while the latter is significantly absent. Material prosperity may easily blind the eyes of church leaders, so much so that they will make it a substitute for spiritual prosperity. How great the need to watch at that point! Prosperity in money matters does not signify growth in holiness. The seasons of material prosperity are rarely seasons of spiritual advance, either to the individual or to the church. It is so easy to lose sight of God when goods increase. It so easy to lean on human agencies and cease praying and relying upon God when material prosperity comes to the church.

If it be contended that the work of God is progressing, and that we are growing in holiness, then some perplexing questions arise which will be hard to answer. If the church is making advances on the lines of deep spirituality—if we are a praying people, noted for our prayer habits—if our people are hungering after holiness—then let us ask, why do we now have so few mighty outpourings of the Holy Spirit on our chief churches and our principal appointments? Why is it that so few of our revivals spring from the life of the pastor who is noted for his deep spirituality, or the life of our church? Is the Lord's hand shortened that he cannot save? Is his ear heavy that he cannot hear? Why is it that in order to have so-called revivals, we must have outside pressure, by the reputation and sensation of some renowned evangelist? This is largely true in our larger charges and with our leading men. Why is it that the pastor is not sufficiently spiritual, holy, and in communion with God, that he cannot hold his own revival services, and have large outpourings of the Holy Spirit on the church, the community and upon himself? There can be but one solution for all this state of things. We have cultivated other things to the neglect of the work of holiness. We have permitted our minds to be preoccupied with material things in the church. Unfortunately, whether designedly or not, we have substituted the external for the internal. We have put that which is seen to the front and shut out that which is unseen. It is all too true as to the church, that we are much further advanced in material matters than in matters spiritual.

But the cause of this sad state of things may be traced further back. It is largely due to the decay of prayer. For with the decline of the work of holiness there has come the decline of the business of praying. As praying and holiness go together, so the decline of one, means the decay of the other. Excuse it if we may, justify the present state of things if we will, yet it is all too patent that the emphasis in the work of the present-day church is not put on prayer. And just as this has occurred, the emphasis has been taken from the great work of God set on foot in the atonement, holiness of heart and life. The church is not turning out praying men and women, because the church is not intently engaged in the one great work of holiness.

At one time, John Wesley saw that there was a perceptible decline in the work of holiness, and he stopped short to inquire into the cause, and if we are as honest and spiritual as he was, we will now see the same causes operating to stay God's work among us. In a letter to his brother, Charles, at one time, he comes directly to the point, and makes short, incisive work of it. Here is how he begins his letter:

> What has hindered the work? I want to consider this. And must we not first say, we are the chief. If we were more holy in heart and life, thoroughly devoted to God, would not all the preachers catch fire, and carry it with them, throughout the land?
>
> Is not the next hindrance the littleness of grace (rather than of gifts) in a considerable part of our preachers? They have not the whole mind that was in Christ. They do not steadily walk as he walked. And, therefore, the hand of the Lord is stayed, though not altogether; though he does work still. But it is not in such a degree as he surely would, were they holy as he that hath sent them is holy.
>
> Is not the third hindrance the littleness of grace in the generality of our people? Therefore, they pray little, and with little fervency for a general blessing. And, therefore, their prayer has little power with God. It does not, as once, shut and open heaven.

Add to this, that as there is much of the spirit of the world in their hearts, so there is much conformity to the world in their lives. They ought to be bright and shining lights, but they neither burn nor shine. They are not true to the rules they profess to observe. They are not holy in all manner of conversation. Nay, many of them are salt that has lost its savor, the little savor they once had. Wherewith then shall the rest of the land be seasoned? What wonder that their neighbors are as unholy as ever?

He strikes the spot. He hits the center. He grades the cause. He freely confesses that he and Charles are the first cause, in this decline of holiness. The chief ones occupy positions of responsibility. As they go, so goes the church. They give color to the church. They largely determine its character and its work. What holiness should mark these chief men? What zeal should ever characterize them? What prayerfulness should be seen in them! How influential they ought to be with God! If the head be weak, then the whole body will feel the stroke.

The pastors come next in his catalogue. When the chief shepherds and those who are under them, the immediate pastors, stay their advance in holiness, the panic will reach to the end of the line. As are the pastors, so will the people be as a rule. If the pastors are prayerless, then will the people follow in their footsteps. If the preacher be silent upon the work of holiness, then will there be no hungering and thirsting after holiness in the laymen. If the preacher be careless about obtaining the highest and best God has for him in religious experience, then will the people take after him.

One statement of Wesley needs to be repeated with emphasis. The littleness of grace rather than the smallness of gifts—this is largely the case with the preachers. It may be stated as an axiom: That the work of God fails as a general rule, more for the lack of grace, than for the want of gifts. It is more than this. It is more than this, for a full supply of grace brings an increase of gifts. It may be repeated that small results, a low experience, a low religious life, and pointless, powerless preaching always flow from a lack of grace. And a lack of grace flows from a lack of praying. Great grace comes from great praying.

What is our calling's glorious hope
But inward holiness?
For this to Jesus I look up,
I calmly wait for this.
I wait till he shall touch me clean,
Shall life and power impart;
Give me the faith that casts out sin,
And purifies the heart.

In carrying on his great work in the world, God works through human agents. He works through his church collectively and through his people individually. In order that they may be effective agents, they must be "vessels unto honor, sanctified, and meet for the master's use, and prepared unto every good work." God works most effectively through holy men. His work makes progress in the hands of praying men. Peter tells us that husbands who might not be reached by the Word of God, might be won by the conduct of their wives. It is those who are "blameless and harmless, the sons of God," who can hold forth the word of life "in the midst of a crooked and perverse nation."

The world judges religion not by what the Bible says, but by how Christians live. Christians are the Bible which sinners read. These are the epistles to be read of all men. "By their fruits ye shall know them." The emphasis, then, is to be placed upon holiness of life. But unfortunately in the present-day church, emphasis has been placed elsewhere. In selecting church workers and choosing ecclesiastical officers, the quality of holiness is not considered. The praying fitness seems not to be taken into account, when it was just otherwise in all of God's movements and in all of his plans. He looked for holy men, those noted for their praying habits. Prayer leaders are scarce. Prayer conduct is not counted as the highest qualification for offices in the church.

We cannot wonder that so little is accomplished in the great work in the world which God has in hand. The fact is that it is surprising so much has been done with such feeble, defective agents. "Holiness to the Lord" needs again to be written on the banners of the church. Once more it needs to be sounded out in the ears of modern Christians. "Follow peace with all men, and holiness, without which no man shall see the Lord."

Let it be emphasized and reemphasized that this is the divine standard of religion. Nothing short of this will satisfy the divine requirement. O the danger of deception at this point! How near one can come to being right and yet be wrong! Some men can come very near to pronouncing the test word, "Shibboleth," but they miss it. "Many will say unto me, Lord, Lord, in that day," says Jesus Christ, but he further states that then will he say unto them, "I never knew you; depart from me, ye that work iniquity."

Men can do many good things and yet not be holy in heart and righteous in conduct. They can do many good things and lack that spiritual quality of heart called holiness. How great the need of hearing the words of Paul guarding us against self-deception in the great work of personal salvation:

> Be not deceived; God is not mocked: for whatsoever a man soweth, that shall he also reap (Gal. 6:7).

> O may I still from sin depart;
> A wise and understanding heart,
> Jesus, to me to be given;
> And let me through thy Spirit know
> To glorify my God below,
> And find my way to heaven.

8

Prayer and Consecration

WHEN we study the many-sidedness of prayer, we are surprised at the number of things with which it is connected.
There is no phase of human life which it does not affect, and it
has to do with everything affecting human salvation. Prayer and
consecration are closely related. Prayer leads up to, and governs
consecration. Prayer is precedent to consecration, accompanies
it, and is a direct result of it. Much goes under the name of consecration which has no consecration in it. Much consecration
of the present day is defective, superficial and spurious, worth
nothing so far as the office and ends of consecration are concerned. Popular consecration is sadly at fault because it has little
or no prayer in it. No consecration is worth a thought which is
not the direct fruit of much praying, and which fails to bring
one into a life of prayer. Prayer is the one thing prominent in a
consecrated life.

Consecration is much more than a life of so-called service. It
is a life of personal holiness, first of all. It is that which brings
spiritual power into the heart and enlivens the entire inner man.
It is a life which ever recognizes God, and a life given up to true
prayer.

Full consecration is the highest type of a Christian life. It is
the one divine standard of experience, of living and of service. It

is the one thing at which the believer should aim. Nothing short of entire consecration must satisfy him.

Never is he to be contented till he is fully, entirely the Lord's by his own consent. His praying naturally and voluntarily leads up to this one act of his.

Consecration is the voluntary set dedication of one's self to God, an offering definitely made, and made without any reservation whatever. It is the setting apart of all we are, all we have, and all we expect to have or be, to God first of all. It is not so much the giving of ourselves to the church, or the mere engaging in some one line of church work. Almighty God is in view and he is the end of all consecration. It is a separation of one's self to God, a devotement of all that he is and has to a sacred use. Some things may be devoted to a special purpose, but it is not consecration in the true sense. Consecration has a sacred nature. It is devoted to holy ends. It is the voluntary putting of one's self in God's hands to be used sacredly, holily, with sanctifying ends in view.

Consecration is not so much the setting one's self apart from sinful things and wicked ends, but rather it is the separation from worldly, secular, and even legitimate things, if they come in conflict with God's plans, to holy uses. It is the devoting of all we have to God for his own specific use. It is a separation from things questionable, or even legitimate, when the choice is to be made between the things of this life and the claims of God.

The consecration which meets God's demands and which he accepts is to be full, complete, with no mental reservation, with nothing withheld. It cannot be partial, any more than a whole burnt offering in Old Testament times could have been partial. The whole animal had to be offered in sacrifice. To reserve any part of the animal would have seriously vitiated the offering. So to make a half-hearted, partial consecration is to make no consecration at all, and is to fail utterly in securing the divine acceptance. It involves our whole being, all we have and all that we are. Everything is definitely and voluntarily placed in God's hands for his supreme use.

Consecration is not all there is in holiness. Many make serious mistakes at this point. Consecration makes us relatively holy. We are holy only in the sense that we are now closely related to God, in which we were not related heretofore. Consecration is the human side of holiness. In this sense, it is self-sanctification, and only in this sense. Sanctification or holiness in its truest and highest sense is divine, the act of the Holy Spirit working in the heart, making it clean and putting therein in a higher degree the fruits of the Spirit.

This distinction is clearly set forth and kept in view by Moses in Leviticus, wherein he shows the human and the divine side of sanctification or holiness:

> Sanctify yourselves, therefore, and be ye holy, for I am the Lord your God. And ye shall keep my statutes and do them; I am the Lord which sanctify you (Lev. 11:44).

Here we are to sanctify ourselves, and then in the next word we are taught that it is the Lord which sanctifies us. God does not consecrate us to his service. We do not sanctify ourselves in this highest sense. Here is the twofold meaning of sanctification, and a distinction which needs to be always kept in mind.

Consecration being the intelligent, voluntary act of the believer, this act is the direct result of praying. No prayerless man ever conceives the idea of a full consecration. Prayerlessness and consecration have nothing whatever in common. A life of prayer naturally leads up to full consecration. It leads nowhere else. In fact, a life of prayer is satisfied with nothing else but an entire dedication of one's self to God. Consecration recognizes fully God's ownership of us. It cheerfully assents to the truth set forth by Paul:

> Ye are not your own. For ye are bought with a price. Therefore, glorify God in your body and spirit, which are God's (1 Cor. 6:19–20).

And true praying leads that way. It cannot reach any other destination. It is bound to run into this depot. This is its natural result. This is the sort of work which praying turns out. Praying makes consecrated people. It cannot make any other sort. It drives to this end. It aims at this very purpose.

As prayer leads up to and brings forth full consecration, so prayer entirely impregnates a consecrated life. The prayer life and the consecrated life are intimate companions. They are Siamese twins, inseparable. Prayer enters into every phase of a consecrated life. A prayerless life which claims consecration is a misnomer, false, counterfeit.

Consecration is really the setting apart of one's self to a life of prayer. It means not only to pray, but to pray habitually, and to pray more effectually. It is the consecrated man who accomplishes most by his praying. God must hear the man wholly given up to God. God cannot deny the requests of him who has renounced all claims to himself, and who has wholly dedicated himself to God and his service. This act of the consecrated man puts him "on praying ground and pleading terms" with God. It puts him in reach of God in prayer. It places him where he can get hold of God, and where he can influence God to do things which he would not otherwise do. Consecration brings answers to prayer. God can depend upon consecrated men. God can afford to commit himself in prayer to those who have fully committed themselves to God. He who gives all to God will get all from God. Having given all to God, he can claim all that God has for him.

As prayer is the condition of full consecration, so prayer is the habit, the rule, of him who has dedicated himself wholly to God. Prayer is becoming in the consecrated life. Prayer is no strange thing in such a life. There is a peculiar affinity between prayer and consecration, for both recognize God, both submit to God, and both have their aim and end in God. Prayer is part and parcel of the consecrated life. Prayer is the constant, the inseparable, the intimate companion of consecration. They walk and talk together.

There is much talk today of consecration, and many are termed consecrated people who know not the alphabet of it. Much modern consecration falls far below the scriptural standard. There is really no real consecration in it. Just as there is much praying without any real prayer in it, so there is much so-called consecration current, today, in the church which has no real consecration in it. Much passes for consecration in the church which receives the praise and plaudits of superficial, formal professors, but which is wide of the mark. There is much hurrying to and fro, here and there, much fuss and feathers, much going about and doing many things, and those who busy themselves after this fashion are called consecrated men and women. The central trouble with all this false consecration is that there is no prayer in it, nor is it in any sense the direct result of praying. People can do many excellent and commendable things in the church and be utter strangers to a life of consecration, just as they can do many things and be prayerless.

Here is the true test of consecration. It is a life of prayer. Unless prayer is preeminent, unless prayer is to the front, the consecration is faulty, deceptive, falsely named. Does he pray? That is the test. A question of every so-called consecrated man. Is he a man of prayer? No consecration is worth a thought if it be devoid of prayer. Yea, more—if it be not preeminently and primarily a life of prayer.

God wants consecrated men because they can pray and will pray. He can use consecrated men because he can use praying men. As prayerless men are in his way, hinder him, and prevent the success of his cause, so likewise unconsecrated men are useless to him, and hinder him in carrying out his gracious plans, and in executing his noble purposes in redemption. God wants consecrated men because he wants praying men. Consecration and prayer meet in the same man. Prayer is the tool with which the consecrated man works. Consecrated men are the agents through whom prayer works. Prayer helps the consecrated man in maintaining his attitude of consecration, keeps him alive to God, and aids him in doing the work to which he is called and to which he has given himself. Consecration helps to effectual praying. Consecration enables one to get the most out of his praying.

> Let him to whom we now belong
> His sovereign right assert;
> And take up every thankful song,
> And every loving heart.

> He justly claims us for his own,
> Who bought us with a price;
> The Christian lives to Christ alone,
> To Christ alone he dies.

We must insist upon it that the prime purpose of consecration is not service in the ordinary sense of that word. Service in the minds of not a few means nothing more than engaging in some of the many forms of modern church activities. There are a multitude of such activities, enough to engage the time and mind of any one, yea, even more than enough. Some of these may be good, others not so good. The present-day church is filled with machinery, organizations, committees and societies, so much so that the power it has is altogether insufficient to run the machinery, or to furnish life sufficient to do all this external work. Consecration has a much higher and nobler end than merely to expend itself in these external things.

Consecration aims at the right sort of service—the scriptural kind. It seeks to serve God, but in entirely a different sphere than that which is in the minds of present-day church leaders and workers. The very first sort of service mentioned by Zacharias, father of John the Baptist, in his wonderful prophecy and statement in Luke 1:74–75, was thus:

> That he would grant unto us, that we being delivered out of the hand of our enemies, might serve him without fear, in holiness and righteousness before him, all the days of our life.

Here we have the idea of "serving God in holiness and righteousness all the days of our life."

And the same kind of service is mentioned in Luke's strong tribute to the father and mother of John the Baptist before the latter's birth:

> And they were both righteous before God, walking in all the commandments and ordinances of the Lord blameless (Luke 1:6).

And Paul, in writing to the Philippians, strikes the same keynote in putting the emphasis on blamelessness of life:

Do all things without murmurings and disputings: that ye may be blameless and harmless, the sons of God, without rebuke, in the midst of a crooked and perverse nation, among whom ye shine as lights in the world; holding forth the word of life (Phil. 2:14–16).

We must mention a truth which is strangely overlooked in these days by what are called personal workers, that in the Epistles of Paul and others, it is not what are called church activities which are brought to the front, but rather the personal life. It is good behavior, righteous conduct, holy living, godly conversation, right tempers—things which belong primarily to the personal life in religion. Everywhere this is emphasized, put in the forefront, made much of and insisted on. Religion first of all puts one to living right. Religion shows itself in the life. Thus is religion to prove its reality, its sincerity and its divinity.

> So let our lips and lives express
> The holy gospel we profess;
> So let our works and virtues shine
> To prove the doctrine all divine.
>
> Thus shall we best proclaim abroad
> The honors of our Savior God;
> When the salvation reigns within
> And grace subdues the power of sin.

The first great end of consecration is holiness of heart and of life. It is to glorify God, and this can be done in no more effectual way than by a holy life flowing from a heart cleansed from all sin. The great burden of heart pressed on every one who becomes a Christian lies right here. This he is to ever keep in mind, and to further this kind of life and this kind of heart, he is to watch, to pray, and to bend all his diligence in using all the means of grace. He who is truly and fully consecrated, lives a holy life. He seeks after holiness of heart, and is not satisfied without it. For this very purpose he consecrates himself to God. He gives himself entirely over to God in order to be holy in heart and in life.

As holiness of heart and of life is thoroughly impregnated with prayer, so consecration and prayer are closely allied in personal religion. It takes prayer to bring one into such a consecrated life of holiness to the Lord, and it takes prayer to maintain such a life. Without much prayer, such a life of holiness will break down. Holy people are praying people. Holiness of heart and life puts people to praying. Consecration puts people to praying in earnest.

Prayerless people are strangers to anything like holiness of heart and cleanness of heart. Those who are unfamiliar with the closet are not at all interested in consecration and holiness. Holiness thrives in the place of secret prayer. The environments of the closet of prayer are favorable to its being and its culture. In the closet holiness is found. Consecration brings one into holiness of heart, and prayer stands hard by when it is done.

The spirit of consecration is the spirit of prayer. The law of consecration is the law of prayer. Both laws work in perfect harmony without the slightest jar or discord. Consecration is the practical expression of true prayer. People who are consecrated are known by their praying habits. Consecration thus expresses itself in prayer. He who is not interested in prayer has no interest in consecration. Prayer creates an interest in consecration, then prayer brings one into a state of heart where consecration is a subject of delight, bringing joy of heart, satisfaction of soul, contentment of spirit. The consecrated soul is the happiest soul. There is no friction whatever between him who is fully given over to God and God's will. There is perfect harmony between the will of such a man and God, and his will. And the two wills being in perfect accord, this brings rest of soul, absence of friction, and the presence of perfect peace.

> Lord, in the strength of grace,
> With a glad heart and free,
> Myself, my residue of days,
> I consecrate to thee.
>
> Thy ransomed servant, I
> Restore to thee thy own;
> And from this moment, live or die,
> To serve my God alone.

9

Prayer and a Definite Religious Standard

MUCH of the feebleness, barrenness, and paucity of religion results from the failure to have a scriptural and reasonable standard in religion, by which to shape character and measure results; and this largely results from the omission of prayer or the failure to put prayer in the standard. We cannot possibly mark our advances in religion if there is no point to which we are definitely advancing. Always there must be something definite before the mind's eye at which we are aiming and to which we are driving. We cannot contrast shapeliness with unshapeliness if there be no pattern after which to model. Neither can there be inspiration if there be no high end to stimulate us.

Many Christians are disjointed and aimless because they have no pattern before them after which conduct and character are to be shaped. They just move on aimlessly, their minds in a cloudy state, no pattern in view, no point in sight, no standard after which they are striving. There is no standard by which to value and gauge their efforts. No magnet is there to fill their eyes, quicken their steps, and to draw them and keep them steady.

All this vague idea of religion grows out of loose notions about prayer. That which helps to make the standard of religion

clear and definite is prayer. That which aids in placing that
standard high is prayer. The praying ones are those who have
something definite in view. In fact prayer itself is a very definite
thing, aims at something specific, and has a mark at which it
aims. Prayer aims at the most definite, the highest and the
sweetest religious experience. The praying ones want all that
God has in store for them. They are not satisfied with anything
like a low religious life, superficial, vague and indefinite. The
praying ones are not only after a "deeper work of grace," but
want the very deepest work of grace possible and promised.
They are not after being saved from some sin, but saved from
all sin, both inward and outward. They are after not only deliverance from sinning, but from sin itself, from its being, its
power and its pollution. They are after holiness of heart and life.

Prayer believes in, and seeks for the very highest religious life
set before us in the Word of God. Prayer is the condition of that
life. Prayer points out the only pathway to such a life. The standard of a religious life is the standard of prayer. Prayer is so
vital, so essential, so far-reaching, that it enters into all religion,
and sets the standard clear and definite before the eye. The
degree of our estimate of prayer fixes our ideas of the standard
of a religious life. The standard of biblical religion is the standard of prayer. The more there is of prayer in the life, the more
definite and the higher our notions of religion.

The Scriptures alone make the standard of life and experience. When we make our own standard, there is delusion and
falsity for our desires, convenience and pleasure form the rule,
and that is always a fleshly and a low rule. From it, all the fundamental principles of a Christlike religion are left out.
Whatever standard of religion which makes in it provision for
the flesh, is unscriptural and hurtful.

Nor will it do to leave it to others to fix the standard of religion for us. When we allow others to make our standard of religion, it is generally deficient because in imitation, defects are
transferred to the imitator more readily than virtues, and a second edition of a man is marred by its defects.

The most serious damage in thus determining what religion
is by what others say, is in allowing current opinion, the contagion of example, the grade of religion current among us, to

shape our religious opinions and characters. Adoniram Judson once wrote to a friend, "Let me beg you, not to rest contented with the commonplace religion that is now so prevalent."

Commonplace religion is pleasing to flesh and blood. There is no self-denial in it, no cross bearing, no self-crucifixion. It is good enough for our neighbors. Why should we be singular and straight-laced? Others are living on a low plane, on a compromising level, living as the world lives. Why should we be peculiar, zealous of good works? Why should we fight to win heaven while so many are sailing there on "flowery beds of ease"? Are the easy-going, careless, sauntering crowd, living prayerless lives, going to heaven? Is heaven a fit place for non-praying, loose living, ease loving people? That is the supreme question.

Paul gives the following caution about making for ourselves the jolly, pleasure-seeking religious company all about us the standard of our measurement:

> For we dare not make ourselves of the number, or compare ourselves with some that commend themselves; but they measuring themselves by themselves, and comparing themselves among themselves, are not wise. But we will not boast of things without our measure, but according to the measure of the rule which God hath distributed to us, a measure to reach even unto you (2 Cor. 10:12–13).

No standard of religion is worth a moment's consideration which leaves prayer out of the account. No standard is worth any thought which does not make prayer the main thing in religion. So necessary is prayer, so fundamental in God's plan, so all important to everything like a religious life, that it enters into all biblical religion. Prayer itself is a standard, definite, emphatic, scriptural. A life of prayer is the divine rule. This is the pattern, just as our Lord, being a man of prayer, is the one pattern for us after whom to copy. Prayer fashions the pattern of a religious life. Prayer is the measure. Prayer molds the life.

The vague, indefinite, popular view of religion has no prayer in it. In its program, prayer is entirely left out or put so low down and made so insignificant, that it hardly is worth mentioning. Man's standard of religion has no prayer about it.

It is God's standard at which we are to aim, not man's. It is not the opinions of men, not what they say, but what the Scriptures say. Loose notions of religion grow out of low notions of prayer. Prayerlessness begets loose, cloudy, and indefinite views of what religion is. Aimless living and prayerlessness go hand in hand. Prayer sets something definite in the mind. Prayer seeks after something specific. The more definite our views as to the nature and need of prayer, the more definite will be our views of Christian experience and right living, and the less vague our views of religion. A low standard of religion lives hard by a low standard of praying.

Everything in a religious life depends upon being definite. The definiteness of our religious experiences and of our living will depend upon the definiteness of our views of what religion is and of the things of which it consists.

The Scriptures ever set before us the one standard of full consecration to God. This is the divine rule. This is the human side of this standard. The sacrifice acceptable to God must be a complete one, entire, a whole burnt offering. This is the measure laid down in God's Word. Nothing less than this can be pleasing to God. Nothing half-hearted can please him. "A living sacrifice," holy, and perfect in all its parts, is the measurement of our service to God. A full renunciation of self, a free recognition of God's right to us, and a sincere offering of all to him—this is the divine requirement. Nothing indefinite in that. Nothing is in that which is governed by the opinions of others or affected by how men live about us.

And while a life of prayer is embraced in such a full consecration, at the same time prayer leads up to the point where a complete consecration is made to God. Consecration is but the silent expression of prayer. And the highest religious standard is the measure of prayer and self-dedication to God. The prayer life and the consecrated life are partners in religion. They are so closely allied they are never separated. The prayer life is the direct fruit of entire consecration to God. Prayer is the natural outflow of a really consecrated life. The measure of consecration is the measure of real prayer. No consecration is pleasing to God which is not perfect in all its parts, just as no burnt offering of a Jew was

ever acceptable to God unless it was a "whole burnt offering."
And a consecration of this sort, after this divine measurement, has
in it as a basic principle, the business of praying. Consecration is
made to God. Prayer has to do with God. Consecration is putting
one's self entirely at the disposal of God. And God wants and
commands all his consecrated ones to be praying ones. This is the
one definite standard at which we must aim. Lower than this we
cannot afford to seek.

A scriptural standard of religion includes a clear religious
experience. Religion is nothing if not experiential. Religion
appeals to the inner consciousness. It is an experience if anything at all, and an experience in addition to a religious life.
There is the internal part of religion as well as the external. Not
only are we to "work out our salvation with fear and trembling,"
but "it is God that worketh in us to will and do of his good pleasure." There is a "good work in you," as well as a life outside to
be lived. The new birth is a definite Christian experience, proved
by infallible marks, appealing to the inner consciousness. The
witness of the Spirit is not an indefinite, vague something, but is
a definite, clear inward assurance given by the Holy Spirit that
we are the children of God. In fact everything belonging to religious experience is clear and definite, bringing conscious joy,
peace and love. And this is the divine standard of religion, a standard attained by earnest, constant prayer, and a religious experience kept alive and enlarged by the same means of prayer.

An end to be gained, to which effort is to be directed, is
important in every pursuit in order to give unity, energy, and
steadiness to it. In the Christian life, such an end is all important. Without a high standard before us to be gained, for which
we are earnestly seeking, lassitude will unnerve effort, and past
experience will taint or exhale into mere sentiment, or be hardened into cold, loveless principle.

We must go on. "Therefore, leaving the principles of the doctrine of Christ, let us go on unto perfection." The present
ground we occupy must be held by making advances, and all
the future must be covered and brightened by it. In religion, we
must not only go on. We must know where we are going. This
is all important. It is essential that in going on in religious expe-

rience, we have something definite in view, and strike out for that one point. To ever go on and not to know to which place we are going, is altogether too vague and indefinite, and is like a man who starts out on a journey and does not have any destination in view. It is important that we not lose sight of the starting point in a religious life, and that we measure the steps already trod. But it is likewise necessary that the end be kept in view and that the steps necessary to reach the standard be always in sight.

10

Prayer Born of Compassion

WE speak here more particularly of spiritual compassion, that which is born in a renewed heart, and which finds hospitality there. This compassion has in it the quality of mercy, is of the nature of pity, and moves the soul with tenderness of feeling for others. Compassion is moved at the sight of sin, sorrow, and suffering. It stands at the other extreme to indifference of spirit to the wants and woes of others, and is far removed from insensibility and hardness of heart, in the midst of want and trouble and wretchedness. Compassion stands beside sympathy for others, is interested in them, and is concerned about them.

That which excites and develops compassion and puts it to work, is the sight of multitudes in want and distress, and helpless to relieve themselves. Helplessness especially appeals to compassion. Compassion is silent but does not remain secluded. It goes out at the sight of trouble, sin, and need. Compassion runs out in earnest prayer, first of all, for those for whom it feels, and has a sympathy for them. Prayer for others is born of a sympathetic heart. Prayer is natural and almost spontaneous when compassion is begotten in the heart. Prayer belongs to the compassionate man.

There is a certain compassion which belongs to the natural man, which expends its force in simple gifts to those in need, not to be despised. But spiritual compassion, the kind born in a renewed heart, which is Christlike in its nature, is deeper, broader, and more prayerlike. Christlike compassion always moves to prayer. This sort of compassion goes beyond the relief of mere bodily wants, and saying, "Be ye warmed—be ye clothed." It reaches deeper down and goes much farther.

Compassion is not blind. Rather we should say, that compassion is not born of blindness. He who has compassion of soul has eyes, first of all, to see the things which excite compassion. He who has no eyes to see the exceeding sinfulness of sin, the wants and woes of humanity, will never have compassion for humanity. It is written of our Lord that "when he saw the multitudes, he was moved with compassion on them." First, seeing the multitudes, with their hunger, their woes and their helpless condition, then compassion. Then prayer for the multitudes. Hard is he, and far from being Christlike, who sees the multitudes, and is unmoved at the sight of their sad state, their unhappiness and their peril. He has no heart of prayer for men.

Compassion may not always move men, but is always moved toward men. Compassion may not always turn men to God, but it will, and does, turn God to man. And where it is most helpless to relieve the needs of others, it can at least break out into prayer to God for others. Compassion is never indifferent, selfish, and forgetful of others. Compassion has alone to do with others. The fact that the multitudes were as sheep having no shepherd, was the one thing which appealed to our Lord's compassionate nature. Then their hunger moved him, and the sight of the sufferings and diseases of these multitudes stirred the pity of his heart.

> Father of mercies, send thy grace
> All powerful from above,
> To form in our obedient souls
> The image of thy love.
>
> O may our sympathizing breasts
> That generous pleasure know;
> Kindly to share in others' joy,
> And weep for others' woe.

But compassion has not alone to do with the body and its disabilities and needs. The soul's distressing state, its needs and danger all appeal to compassion. The highest state of grace is known by the infallible mark of compassion for poor sinners. This sort of compassion belongs to grace, and sees not alone the bodies of men, but their immortal spirits, soiled by sin, unhappy in their condition without God, and in imminent peril of being forever lost. When compassion beholds this sight of dying men hurrying to the bar of God, then it is that it breaks out into intercessions for sinful men. Then it is that compassion speaks out after this fashion:

> But feeble my compassion proves,
> And can but weep where most it loves;
> Thy own all saving arm employ,
> And turn these drops of grief to joy.

The prophet Jeremiah declares this about God, giving the reason why sinners are not consumed by his wrath:

> It is of the Lord's mercies that we are not consumed, because his compassions fail not (Lam. 3:22).

And it is this divine quality in us which makes us so much like God. So we find the psalmist describing the righteous man who is pronounced blessed by God: "He is gracious and full of compassion, and righteous."

And as giving great encouragement to penitent praying sinners, the psalmist thus records some of the striking attributes of the divine character: "The Lord is gracious and full of compassion, slow to anger, and of great mercy."

It is no wonder, then, that we find it recorded several times of our Lord while on earth that "he was moved with compassion." Can any one doubt that his compassion moved him to pray for those suffering, sorrowing ones who came across his pathway?

Paul was wonderfully interested in the religious welfare of his Jewish brethren, was concerned over them, and his heart was strangely warmed with tender compassion for their salvation, even though mistreated and sorely persecuted by them. In writing to the Romans, we hear him thus express himself:

> I say the truth in Christ, I lie not, my conscience also bearing me witness in the Holy Ghost, that I have great heaviness and

continual sorrow in my heart. For I could wish that myself were accursed from Christ for my brethren, my kinsmen according to the flesh (Rom. 9:1–3).

What marvelous compassion is here described for Paul's own nation! What wonder that a little later on he records his desire and prayer:

Brethren, my heart's desire and prayer to God for Israel is, that they might be saved (Rom. 10:1).

We have an interesting case in Matthew which gives us an account of what excited so largely the compassion of our Lord at one time:

But when he saw the multitudes, he was moved with compassion on them, because they fainted, and were scattered abroad, as sheep having no shepherd. Then saith he unto his disciples, The harvest truly is plenteous, but the labourers are few; Pray ye therefore the Lord of the harvest, that he will send forth labourers into his harvest (Matt. 9:36–38).

It seems from parallel statements that our Lord had called his disciples aside to rest awhile, exhausted as he and they were by the excessive demands on them, by the ceaseless contact with the persons who were ever coming and going, and by their exhaustive toil in ministering to the immense multitudes. But the multitudes precede him, and instead of finding wilderness solitude, quiet and repose, he finds great multitudes eager to see and hear, and to be healed. His compassions are moved. The ripened harvests need laborers. He did not call these laborers at once, by sovereign authority, but charges the disciples to betake themselves to God in prayer, asking him to send forth laborers into his harvest.

Here is the urgency of prayer enforced by the compassions of our Lord. It is prayer born of compassion for perishing humanity. Prayer is pressed on the church for laborers to be sent into the harvest of the Lord. The harvest will go to waste and perish without the laborers, while the laborers must be God-chosen, God-sent, and God-commissioned. But God does not send these laborers.

into his harvest without prayer. The failure of the laborers is owing to the failure of prayer. The scarcity of laborers in the harvest is due to the fact that the church fails to pray for laborers according to his command.

The ingathering of the harvests of earth for the granaries of heaven is dependent on the prayers of God's people. Prayer secures the laborers sufficient in quantity and in quality for all the needs of the harvest. God's chosen laborers, God's endowed laborers, and God's thrust-forth laborers, are the only ones who will truly go, filled with Christlike compassion and endued with Christlike power, whose going will avail, and these are secured by prayer. Christ's people on their knees with Christ's compassion in their hearts for dying men and for needy souls, exposed to eternal peril, is the pledge of laborers in numbers and character to meet the wants of earth and the purposes of heaven.

God is sovereign of the earth and of heaven, and the choice of laborers in his harvest he delegates to no one else. Prayer honors him as sovereign and moves him to his wise and holy selection. We will have to put prayer to the front ere the fields of paganism will be successfully tilled for Christ. God knows his men, and he likewise knows full well his work. Prayer gets God to send forth the best men and the most fit men and the men best qualified to work in the harvest. Moving the missionary cause by forces this side of God has been its bane, its weakness, and its failure. Compassion for the world of sinners, fallen in Adam but redeemed in Christ, will move the church to pray for them and stir the church to pray the Lord of the harvest to send forth laborers into the harvest.

> Lord of the harvest, hear
> Thy needy servants' cry;
> Answer our faith's effectual prayer,
> And all our wants supply.
>
> Convert and send forth more
> Into thy church abroad;
> And let them speak thy word of power,
> As workers with their God.

What a comfort and what hope there is to fill our breasts when we think of one in heaven who ever lives to intercede for us, because "His compassion fails not!" Above everything else, we have a compassionate Savior, one "who can have compassion on the ignorant, and on them who are out of the way, for that he himself is compassed about with infirmity." The compassion of our Lord well fits him for being the great high priest of Adam's fallen, lost, and helpless race.

And if he is filled with such compassion that it moves him at the Father's right hand to intercede for us, then by every token we should have the same compassion on the ignorant and those out of the way, exposed to divine wrath, as would move us to pray for them. Just insofar as we are compassionate will we be prayerful for others. Compassion does not expend its force in simply saying, "Be ye warmed; be ye clothed," but drives us to our knees in prayer for those who need Christ and his grace.

> The Son of God in tears
> The wondering angels see;
> Be thou astonished, O my soul!
> He shed those tears for thee.
>
> He wept that we might weep;
> Each sin demands a tear;
> In heaven alone no sin is found,
> And there's no weeping there.

Jesus Christ was altogether man. While he was the divine Son of God yet at the same time, he was the human Son of God. Christ had a preeminently human side, and, here, compassion reigned. He was tempted in all points as we are, yet without sin. At one time how the flesh seems to have weakened under the fearful strain upon him, and how he must have inwardly shrunk under the pain and pull! Looking up to heaven, he prays, "Father, save me from this hour." How the spirit nerves and holds —"but for this cause came I to this hour." Only he can solve this mystery who has followed his Lord in straits and gloom and pain, and realized that the "spirit is willing but the flesh is weak."

All this but fitted our Lord to be a compassionate Savior. It is no sin to feel the pain and realize the darkness on the path into which God leads. It is only human to cry out against the pain, the terror, and desolation of that hour. It is divine to cry out to God in that hour, even while shrinking and sinking down, "For this cause came I unto this hour." Shall I fail through the weakness of the flesh? No. "Father, glorify thy name." How strong it makes us, and how true, to have one pole star to guide us to the glory of God!

11

Concerted Prayer

THE pious Quesnel says that "God is found in union and agreement. Nothing is more efficacious than this in prayer." Intercessions combine with prayers and supplications. The word does not mean necessarily prayer in relation to others. It means a coming together, a falling in with a most intimate friend for free, unrestrained communion. It implies prayer, free, familiar, and bold.

Our Lord deals with this question of the concert of prayer in the eighteenth chapter of Matthew. He deals with the benefit and energy resulting from the aggregation of prayer forces. The prayer principle and the prayer promise will be best understood in the connection in which it was made by our Lord:

> Moreover if thy brother shall trespass against thee, go and tell him his fault between thee and him alone: if he shall hear thee, thou hast gained thy brother. But if he will not hear thee, then take with thee one or two more, that in the mouth of two or three witnesses every word may be established. And if he shall neglect to hear them, tell it unto the church; but if he neglect to hear the church, let him be unto thee as an heathen man and a publican. Verily I say unto you, Whatsoever ye shall bind on earth shall be bound in heaven; and whatsoever ye shall loose on earth shall be loosed in heaven. Again I say unto you, That if

two of you shall agree on earth as touching any thing that they shall ask, it shall be done for them of my Father which is in heaven. For where two or three are gathered together in my name, there am I in the midst of them (vv. 15–20).

This represents the church in prayer to inforce discipline in order that its members who have been overtaken by faults, may yield readily to the disciplinary process. In addition, it is the church called together in a concert of prayer in order to repair the waste and friction ensuing upon the cutting off of a church offender. This last direction as to a concert of prayer is that the whole matter may be referred to Almighty God for his approval and ratification.

All this means that the main, the concluding, and the all powerful agency in the church is prayer, whether it be, as we have seen in the ninth chapter of Matthew, to thrust out laborers into God's earthly harvest fields, or to exclude from the church a violator of unity, law and order, who will neither listen to his brethren nor repent and confess his fault.

It means that church discipline, now a lost art in the modern church, must go hand in hand with prayer, and that the church which has no disposition to separate wrong-doers from the church, and which has no excommunication spirit for incorrigible offenders against law and order, will have no communication with God. Church purity must precede the church's prayers. The unity of discipline in the church precedes the unity of prayers by the church.

Let it be noted with emphasis that a church which is careless of discipline will be careless in praying. A church which tolerates evildoers in its communion, will cease to pray, will cease to pray with agreement, and will cease to be a church gathered together in prayer in Christ's name.

This matter of church discipline is an important one in the Scriptures. The need of watchfulness over the lives of its members belongs to the church of God. The church is an organization for mutual help, and it is charged with the watch care of all of its members. Disorderly conduct cannot be passed by unnoticed. The course of procedure in such cases is clearly given in the eighteenth chapter of Matthew, which has been heretofore referred to. Furthermore, Paul, in Galatians 6:1, gives explicit directions as to those who fall into sin in the church:

> Brethren, if a man be overtaken in a fault, ye which are spiritual, restore such an one in the spirit of meekness; considering thyself, lest thou also be tempted.

The work of the church is not alone to members but it is to watch over and guard them after they have entered the church. And if any are overtaken by sin, they must be sought out, and if they cannot be cured of their faults, then excision must take place. This is the doctrine our Lord lays down.

It is somewhat striking that the church at Ephesus (Rev. 2), though it had left its first love and had sadly declined in vital godliness and in those things which make up spiritual life, yet receives credit for this good quality: "Thou canst not bear them that are evil."

While the church at Pergamos was admonished because it had there among its membership those who taught such hurtful doctrines that were a stumbling block to others. And not so much that such characters were in the church, but that they were tolerated. The impression is that the church leaders were blind to the presence of such hurtful characters, and hence were indisposed to administer discipline. This indisposition was an unfailing sign of prayerlessness in the membership. There was no union of prayer effort looking to cleansing the church and keeping it clean.

This disciplinary idea stands out prominently in the apostle Paul's writings. The church at Corinth had a notorious case of fornication. A man had an incestuous relationship with his stepmother, and this church had been careless about this iniquity. Paul rather sharply reproved this church and gave explicit command to this effect: "Therefore put away from among yourselves that wicked person." Here was concert of action on the part of praying people demanded by Paul.

As good a church as that at Thessalonica needed instruction and caution on this matter of looking after disorderly persons. So we hear Paul saying to them:

> Now we command you, brethren, in the name of our Lord Jesus Christ, that ye withdraw yourselves from every brother that walketh disorderly (2 Thess. 3:6).

Mark you. It is not the mere presence of disorderly persons in a church which merits the displeasure of God. It is when they are tolerated under the mistaken plea of "bearing with them," and no steps are taken either to cure them of their evil practices or exclude them from the fellowship of the church. And this glaring neglect on the part of the church of its wayward members is but a sad sign of a lack of praying, for a praying church, given to mutual praying, agreement praying, is keen to discern when a brother is overtaken in a fault, and seeks either to restore him, or to cut him off if he be incorrigible.

Much of this dates back to the lack of spiritual vision on the part of church leaders. The Lord by the mouth of the prophet Isaiah once asked the very pertinent, suggestive question, "And who is blind but my servant?" This blindness in leadership in the church is no more patent than in this question of seeing evil-doers in the church, in caring for them, and when the effort to restore them fails, to withdraw fellowship from them and let them be "as a heathen man and a publican." The truth is there is such a lust for members in the church in these modern times, that the officials and preachers have entirely lost sight of the members who have violated baptismal covenants, and who are living in open disregard of God's Word. The idea now is *quantity* in membership, *not quality*. The purity of the church is put in the background in the craze to secure numbers, and to pad the church rolls and make large figures in statistical columns. Prayer, much prayer, mutual prayer, would bring the church back to scriptural standards, and would purge the church of many wrongdoers, while it might cure not a few of their evil lives.

Prayer and church discipline are not new revelations of the Christian dispensation. These two things had a high place in the Jewish church. Instances are too numerous to mention all of them. Ezra is a case in point. When he returned from the captivity, he found a sad and distressing condition of things among the Lord's people who were left in the land. They had not separated themselves from the surrounding heathen people, and had intermarried with them, contrary to divine commands. And those high in the church were involved, the priests and the Levites with others. Ezra was greatly moved at the account given him, and rent his garments and wept and prayed. Evil-doers in the church did not meet his approval, nor did he shut his eyes to them nor excuse them, neither did he compromise the situation. When he had finished confessing the sins of the people and his praying, the people assembled themselves before him and joined him in a covenant agreement to put away from them their evil doings, and wept and prayed in company with Ezra.

The result was that the people thoroughly repented of their transgressions, and Israel was reformed. Praying and a good man, who was neither blind nor unconcerned, did the deed.

Of Ezra it is written, "For he mourned because of the transgression of them that had been carried away." So it is with every praying man in the church when he has eyes to see the transgression of evildoers in the church, who has a heart to grieve over them, and who has a spirit in him so concerned about the church that he prays about it.

Blessed is that church who has praying leaders, who can see that which is disorderly in the church, who are grieved about it, and who put forth their hands to correct the evils which harm God's cause as a weight to its progress. One point in the indictment against those "Who are at ease in Zion," referred to by Amos, is that "they are not grieved for the affliction of Joseph." And this same indictment could be brought against church leaders of modern time. They are not grieved because the members are engulfed in a craze for worldly, carnal things, nor when there are those in the church walking openly in disorder, whose lives scandalize religion. Of course such leaders do not pray over the matter, for praying would beget a spirit of solicitude in them for these evildoers, and would drive away the spirit of unconcern which possesses them.

It would be well for prayerless church leaders and careless pastors to read the account of the ink horn man in Ezekiel nine, where God instructed the prophet to send through the city certain men who would destroy those in the city because of the great evils found therein. But certain persons were to be spared. These were they who "sigh and cry for all the abominations that be done in the midst of the city." The man with the ink horn was to mark every one of these sighers and mourners so that they would escape the impending destruction. Please note that the instructions were that the slaying of those who did not mourn and sigh should "Begin at my sanctuary."

What a lesson for nonpraying, unconcerned officials of the modern church! How few there are who "sigh and cry" for present abominations in the land, and who are grieved over the desolations of Zion! What need for "two or three to be gathered together" in a concert of prayer over these conditions, and in the secret place weep and pray for the sins in Zion!

This concert of prayer, this agreement in praying, taught by our Lord in the nineteenth chapter of Matthew, finds proof and illustration elsewhere. This was the kind of prayer which Paul referred to in his request to his Roman brethren, recorded in Romans 15:30–31:

> Now I beseech you, brethren, for the Lord Jesus Christ's sake, and for the love of the Spirit, that ye strive together with me in your prayers to God for me; that I may be delivered from them that do not believe in Judea.

Here is unity in prayer, prayer by agreement, and prayer which drives directly at deliverance from unbelieving and evil men, the same kind of prayer urged by our Lord, and the end practically the same, deliverance from unbelieving men, that deliverance wrought either by bringing them to repentance or by exclusion from the church.

The same idea is found in 2 Thessalonians 3:1–2:

> Finally, brethren, pray for us, that the word of the Lord may have free course, and be glorified, even as it is with you; and that we may be delivered from unreasonable and wicked men.

Here is united prayer requested by an apostle, among other things, for deliverance from wicked men, that same that the church of God needs in this day. By joining their prayers to his, there was the desired end of riddance from men who were hurtful to the church of God and who were a hindrance to the running of the Word of the Lord. Let us ask, are there not in the present-day church those who are a positive hindrance to the ongoing of the Word of the Lord? What better course is there than to jointly pray over the question, at the same time using the Christ-given course of discipline first to save them, but failing in that course, to excise them from the body?

Does that seem a harsh course? Then our Lord was guilty of harshness himself, for he ends these directions by saying, "But if he neglect to hear the church, let him be unto thee as a heathen man and a publican."

No more is this harshness than is the art of the skillful surgeon, who sees the whole body and its members endangered by a gangrenous limb, and severs the limb from the body for the good of the whole. No more was it harshness in the captain and crew of the vessel on which Jonah was found, when the storm arose threatening destruction to all on board, to cast the fleeing prophet overboard. What seems harshness is obedience to God, is for the welfare of the church, and is wise in the extreme.

12

The Universality of Prayer

PRAYER is far-reaching in its influence and worldwide in its effects. It affects all men, affects them everywhere, and affects them in all things. It touches man's interest in time and eternity. It lays hold upon God and moves him to interfere in the affairs of earth. It moves the angels to minister to men in this life. It restrains and defeats the devil in his schemes to ruin man. Prayer goes everywhere and lays its hand upon everything. There is a universality in prayer. When we talk about prayer and its work we must use universal terms. It is individual in its application and benefits, but it is general and worldwide at the same time in its good influences. It blesses man in every event of life, furnishes him help in every emergency, and gives him comfort in every trouble. There is no experience through which man is called to go but prayer is there as a helper, a comforter and a guide.

When we speak of the universality of prayer, we discover many sides to it. First, it may be marked that all men ought to pray. Prayer is intended for all men, because all men need God and need what God has and what prayer only can secure. As men are called upon to pray everywhere, by consequence all men must pray, for men are everywhere. Universal terms are used when men are commanded to pray, while there is a promise in universal terms to all who call upon God for pardon, for mercy and for help:

> For there is no difference . . . for the same Lord over all is rich unto all that call upon him. For whosoever shall call upon the name of the Lord shall be saved (Rom. 10:12–13).

93

As there is no difference in the state of sin in which men are found, and all men need the saving grace of God which only can bless them, and as this saving grace is obtained only in answer to prayer, therefore all men are called on to pray because of their very needs.

It is a rule of scriptural interpretation that whenever a command issues with no limitation, it is universal in binding force. So the words of the Lord in Isaiah are to the point:

> Seek ye the Lord while he may be found, call ye upon him while he is near. Let the wicked forsake his way, and the unrighteous man his thoughts: and let him return unto the Lord, and he will have mercy upon him; and to our God, for he will abundantly pardon (Isa. 55:6–7).

So that as wickedness is universal, and as pardon is needed by all men, so all men must seek the Lord while he may be found, and must call upon him while he is near. Prayer belongs to all men because all men are redeemed in Christ. It is a privilege for every man to pray, but it is no less a duty for them to call upon God. No sinner is barred from the mercy seat. All are welcomed to approach the throne of grace with all their wants and woes, with all their sins and burdens.

> Come all the world, come, sinner thou,
> All things in Christ are ready now.

Whenever a poor sinner turns his eyes to God, no matter where he is nor what his guilt and sinfulness, the eye of God is upon him and his ear is opened to his prayers.

But men may pray everywhere, since God is accessible in every clime and under all circumstances. "I will therefore that men pray everywhere, lifting up holy hands, without wrath and doubting."

No locality is too distant from God on earth to reach heaven. No place is so remote that God cannot see and hear one who looks toward him and seeks his face. Oliver Holden puts into a hymn these words:

> Then, my soul, in every strait,
> To thy Father come and wait;
> He will answer every prayer;
> God is present everywhere.

There is just this modification of the idea that one can pray everywhere. Some places, because of the evil business carried on there, or because of the environments which belong there, growing out of the place itself, the moral character of those who carry on the business, and of those who support it, are localities where prayer would not be in place. We might list the saloon, the theater, the opera, the card table, the dance, and other like places of worldly amusement. Prayer is so much out of place at such places that no one would ever presume to pray. Prayer would be an intrusion, so regarded by the owners, the patrons, and the supporters of such places. Furthermore those who attend such places are not praying people. They belong almost entirely to the prayerless crowd of worldlings.

While we are to pray everywhere, it unquestionably means that we are not to frequent places where we cannot pray. To pray everywhere is to pray in all legitimate places, and to attend especially those places where prayer is welcome, and is given a gracious hospitality. To pray everywhere is to preserve the spirit of prayer in places of business, in our intercourse with men, and in the privacy of the home amid all of its domestic cares.

The model prayer of our Lord, called familiarly "The Lord's Prayer," is the universal prayer, because it is peculiarly adapted to all men everywhere in all circumstances in all times of need. It can be put in the mouths of all people in all nations, and in all times. It is a model of praying which needs no amendment nor alteration for every family, people, and nation.

Furthermore, prayer has its universal application in that all men are to be the subjects of prayer. All men everywhere are to be prayed for. Prayer must take in all of Adam's fallen race because all men are fallen in Adam, redeemed in Christ, and are benefited by prayers for them. This is Paul's doctrine in his prayer directory in 1 Timothy 2:1:

I exhort, therefore, that first of all, supplications, prayers, intercessions and giving of thanks be made for all men.

There is strong scriptural warrant, therefore, for reaching out and embracing all men in our prayers, since not only are we commanded thus to pray for them, but the reason given is that Christ gave himself a ransom for all men, and all men are provisionally beneficiaries of the atoning death of Jesus Christ.

But lastly, and more at length, prayer has a universal side in that all things which concern us are to be prayed about, while all things which are for our good, physical, social, intellectual, spiritual, and eternal, are subjects of prayer. Before, however, we consider this phase of prayer let us stop and again look at the universal prayer for all men. As a special class to be prayed for, we may mention those who have control in state or who bear rule in the church. Prayer has mighty potencies. It makes good rulers, and makes them better rulers. It restrains the lawless and the despotic. Rulers are to be prayed for. They are not out of the reach and the control of prayer, because they are not out of the reach and control of God. Wicked Nero was on the throne of Rome when Paul wrote these words to Timothy urging prayer for those in authority.

Christian lips are to breathe prayers for the cruel and infamous rulers in state as well as for the righteous and the benign governors and princes. Prayer is to be as far-reaching as the race, "for all men." Humanity is to burden our hearts as we pray, and all men are to engage our thoughts in approaching a throne of grace. In our praying hours, all men must have a place. The wants and woes of the entire race are to broaden and make tender our sympathies, and inflame our petitions. No little man can pray. No man with narrow views of God, of his plan to save men, and of the universal needs of all men, can pray effectually. It takes a broadminded man, who understands God and his purposes in the atonement, to pray well. No cynic can pray. Prayer is the divinest philanthropy, as well as giant-great-heartedness. Prayer comes from a big heart, filled with thoughts about all men and with sympathies for all men.

Prayer runs parallel with the will of God, "who will have all men to be saved and to come unto the knowledge of the truth."

Prayer reaches up to heaven, and brings heaven down to earth. Prayer has in its hands a double blessing. It rewards him who prays, and blesses him who is prayed for. It brings peace to warring passions and calms warring elements. Tranquility is the happy fruit of true praying. There is an inner calm which comes to him who prays, and an outer calm as well. Prayer creates "quiet and peaceable lives in all godliness and honesty."

Right praying not only makes life beautiful in peace, but redolent in righteousness and weighty in influence. Honesty, gravity, integrity, and weight in character are the natural and essential fruits of prayer.

It is this kind of worldwide, large-hearted, unselfish praying which pleases God well, and which is acceptable in his sight, because it cooperates with his will and runs in gracious streams to all men and to each man. It is this kind of praying which the man Christ Jesus did when on earth, and the same kind which he is now doing at his Father's right hand in heaven, as our mighty intercessor. He is the pattern of prayer. He is between God and man, the one mediator, who gave himself a ransom for all men, and for each man.

So it is that true prayer links itself to the will of God, and runs in streams of solicitude, and compassion, and intercession for all men. As Jesus Christ died for every one involved in the fall, so prayer girdles every one and gives itself for the benefit of every one. Like our one mediator between God and man, he who prays stands midway between God and man, with prayers, supplications, "and strong cryings and tears." Prayer holds in its grasp the movements of the race of man, and embraces the destinies of men for all eternity. The king and the beggar are both affected by it. It touches heaven and moves earth. Prayer holds earth to heaven and brings heaven in close contact with earth.

> Your guides and brethren bear
> Forever on your mind;
> Extend the arms of mighty prayer
> In grasping all mankind.

13

Prayer and Missions

MISSIONS means the giving of the gospel to those of Adam's fallen race who have never heard of Christ and his atoning death. It means the giving to others the opportunity to hear of salvation through our Lord Jesus Christ, and allowing others to have a chance to receive, and accept the blessings of the gospel, as we have it in christianized lands. It means that those who enjoy the benefits of the gospel give these same religious advantages and gospel privileges to all of mankind. Prayer has a great deal to do with missions. Prayer is the handmaid of missions. The success of all real missionary effort is dependent on prayer. The life and spirit of missions are the life and spirit of prayer. Both prayer and missions were born in the divine mind. Prayer and missions are bosom companions. Prayer creates and makes missions successful, while missions lean heavily on prayer. In the seventy-second Psalm, one which deals with the Messiah, it is stated that "prayer shall be made for him continually." Prayer would be made for his coming to save man, and prayer would be made for the success of the plan of salvation which he would come to set on foot.

The Spirit of Jesus Christ is the spirit of missions. Our Lord Jesus Christ was himself the first missionary. His promise and advent composed the first missionary movement. The missionary spirit is not simply a phase of the gospel, not a mere feature of the plan of salvation, but is its very spirit and life. The missionary movement is the church of Jesus Christ marching in militant array, with the design of possessing the whole world of mankind for Christ. Whoever is touched by the Spirit of God is fired by the missionary spirit. An anti-missionary Christian is a contradiction in terms. We might say that it would be impossible to be an anti-missionary Christian because of the impossibility for the divine and human forces to put men in such a state as not to align them with the missionary cause. Missionary impulse is the heart-beat of our Lord Jesus Christ, sending the vital forces of himself through the whole body of the church. The spiritual life of God's people rises or falls with the force of those heartbeats. When these life forces cease, then death ensues. So that anti-missionary churches are dead churches, just as anti-missionary Christians are dead Christians.

The craftiest wile of Satan, if he cannot prevent a great movement for God, is to debauch the movement. If he can put the movement first, and the spirit of the movement in the background, he has materialized and thoroughly debauched the movement. Mighty prayer only will save the movement from being materialized, and keep the spirit of the movement strong and controlling.

The key of all missionary success is prayer. That key is in the hands of the home churches. The trophies won by our Lord in heathen lands will be won by praying missionaries, not by professional workers in foreign lands. More especially will this success be won by saintly praying in the churches at home. The home church on her knees fasting and praying, is the great base of spiritual supplies, the sinews of war, and the pledge of victory in this dire and final conflict. Financial resources are not the real sinews of war in this fight. Machinery in itself carries no power to break down heathen walls, open effectual doors and win heathen hearts to Christ. Prayer alone can do the deed.

Aaron and Hur did not more surely give victory to Israel through Moses, than a praying church through Jesus Christ will give victory on every battlefield in heathen lands. It is as true in foreign fields as it is in home lands. The praying church wins the contest. The home church has done but a paltry thing when she has furnished the money to establish missions and support her missionaries. Money is important, but money without prayer is powerless in the face of the darkness, the wretchedness, and the sin in unchristianized lands. Prayerless giving breeds barrenness and death. Poor praying at home is the solution of poor results in the foreign field. Prayerless giving is the secret of all crises in the missionary movements of the day, and is the occasion of the accumulation of debts in missionary boards.

It is all right to urge men to give of their means to the missionary cause. But it is much more important to urge them to give their prayers to the movement. Foreign missions need, today, more the power of prayer than the power of money. Prayer can make even poverty in the missionary cause move on amidst difficulties and hindrances. Much money without prayer is helpless and powerless in the face of the utter darkness and sin and wretchedness on the foreign field.

This is peculiarly a missionary age. Protestant Christianity is stirred as it never was before in the line of aggression in pagan lands. The missionary movement has taken on proportions that awaken hope, kindle enthusiasm, and which demand the attention, if not the interest, of the coldest and the most lifeless. Nearly every church has caught the contagion, and the sails of their proposed missionary movements are spread wide to catch the favoring breezes. Herein is the danger just now, that the missionary movement will go ahead of the missionary spirit. This has always been the peril of the church, losing the substance in the shade, losing the spirit in the outward shell, and contenting itself in the mere parade of the movement, putting the force of effort in the movement and not in the spirit.

The magnificence of this movement may not only blind us to the spirit of it, but the spirit which should give life and shape to the movement may be lost in the wealth of the movement as the ship, borne by favoring winds, may be lost when these winds swell to a storm.

Not a few of us have heard many eloquent and earnest speeches stressing the imperative need of money for missions where we have heard only one stressing the imperative need of prayer. All our plans and devices drive to the one end of raising money, not to quicken faith and promote prayer. The common idea among church leaders is that if we get the money, prayer will come as a matter of course. The very reverse is the truth. If we get the church at the business of praying, and thus secure the spirit of missions, money will more than likely come as a matter of course. Spiritual agencies and spiritual forces never come as a matter of course. Spiritual duties and spiritual factors, left to the "matter of course" law, will surely fall out and die. Only the things which are stressed live and rule in the spiritual realm. They who give, will not necessarily pray. Many in our churches are liberal givers who are noted for their prayerlessness. One of the evils of the present-day missionary movement lies just there. Giving is entirely removed from prayer. Prayer receives scant attention, while giving stands out prominently. They who truly pray will be moved to give. Praying creates the giving spirit. The praying ones will give liberally and self-denyingly. He who enters his closet to God, will also open his purse to God. But perfunctory, grudging, assessment-giving kills the very spirit of prayer. Emphasizing the material to the neglect of the spiritual, by an inexorable law retires and discounts the spiritual.

It is truly wonderful how great a part money plays in the modern religious movements, and how little prayer plays in them. In striking contrast with that statement, it is marvelous how little a part money played in primitive Christianity as a factor in spreading the gospel, and how wonderful a part prayer played in it.

The grace of giving is nowhere cultured to a richer growth than in the closet. If all our missionary boards and secretaryships were turned into praying bands, until the agony of real prayer and travail with Christ for a perishing world came on them, real estate, bank stocks, United States bonds would be in the market for the spreading of Christ's gospel among men. If the spirit of prayer prevailed, missionary boards whose individual members are worth millions, would not be staggering under a load of debt and great churches would not have a yearly deficit and a yearly grumbling, grudging, and pressure to pay a beggarly assessment to support a mere handful of missionaries, with the additional humiliation of debating the question of recalling some of them. The ongoing of Christ's kingdom is locked up in the closet of prayer by Christ himself, and not in the contribution box.

The prophet Isaiah, looking down the centuries with the vision of a seer, thus expresses his purpose to continue in prayer and give God no rest till Christ's kingdom be established among men:

> For Zion's sake will I not hold my peace, and for Jerusalem's sake I will not rest, until the righteousness thereof go forth as brightness, and the salvation thereof as a lamp that burneth (Isa. 62:1).

Then, foretelling the final success of the Christian church, he thus speaks:

> And the Gentiles shall see thy righteousness, and all kings thy glory: and thou shalt be called by a new name, which the mouth of the Lord shall name (Isa. 62:2).

Then the Lord, himself, by the mouth of this evangelical prophet, declares as follows:

> I have set watchmen upon thy walls, O Jerusalem, which shall never hold their peace day nor night: ye that make mention of the Lord, keep not silence. And give him no rest, till he establish, and till he make Jerusalem a praise in the earth (Isa. 62:6–7).

In the margin of our Bible, it reads, "Ye that are the Lord's remembrances." The idea is, that these praying ones are those who are the Lord's remembrances, those who remind him of what he has promised, and who give him no rest till God's church is established in the earth.

And one of the leading petitions in the Lord's Prayer deals with this same question of the establishing of God's kingdom and the progress of the gospel in the short, pointed petition, "Thy kingdom come," with the added words, "Thy will be done on earth as it is done in heaven."

The missionary movement in the apostolic church was born in an atmosphere of fasting and prayer. The very movement looking to offering the blessings of the Christian church to the Gentiles was on the housetop on the occasion when Peter went up there to pray, and God showed him his divine purpose to extend the privileges of the gospel to the Gentiles, and to break down the middle wall of partition between Jew and Gentile.

But more specifically Paul and Barnabas were definitely called and set apart to the missionary field at Antioch when the church there had fasted and prayed. It was then the Holy Spirit answered from heaven: "Separate me Barnabas and Saul for the work whereunto I have called them."

Please note this was not the call to the ministry of Paul and Barnabas, but more particularly their definite call to the foreign field. Paul had been called to the ministry years before this, even at his conversion. This was a subsequent call to a work born of special and continued prayer in the church at Antioch. God calls men not only to the ministry but to be missionaries. Missionary work is God's work. And it is the God-called men who are to do it. These are the kind of missionaries which have wrought well and successfully in the foreign field in the past, and the same kind will do the work in the future, or it will not be done.

It is praying missionaries who are needed for the work, and it is a praying church who sends them out, which are prophecies of the success which is promised. The sort of religion to be exported by missionaries is of the praying sort. The religion to which the heathen world is to be converted is a religion of prayer, and a religion of prayer to the true God. The heathen world already prays to its idols and false gods. But they are to be taught by praying missionaries, sent out by a praying church, to cast away their idols and to begin to call upon the name of the Lord Jesus Christ. No prayerless church can transport to heathen lands a praying religion. No prayerless missionary can bring heathen idolaters who know not our God to their knees in true prayer until he becomes preeminently a man of prayer. As it takes praying men at home to do God's work, none the less does it take praying missionaries to bring those who sit in darkness to the light.

The most noted and most successful missionaries have been preeminently men of prayer. David Livingstone, William Taylor, Adoniram Judson, Henry Martyn, and Hudson Taylor, with many more, form a band of illustrious praying men whose impress and influence still abide where they labored. No prayerless man is wanted for this job. Above everything else, the primary qualification for every missionary is prayer. Let him be, above everything else, a man of prayer. And when the crowning day comes, and the records are made up and read at the great judgment day, then it will appear how well praying men wrought in the hard fields of heathendom, and how much was due to them in laying the foundations of Christianity in those fields.

The one only condition which is to give worldwide power to this gospel is prayer, and the spread of this gospel will depend on prayer. The energy which was to give it marvelous momentum and conquering power over all its malignant and powerful foes is the energy of prayer.

The fortunes of the kingdom of Jesus Christ are not made by the feebleness of its foes. They are strong and bitter and have ever been strong, and ever will be. But mighty prayer—this is the one great spiritual force which will enable the Lord Jesus Christ to enter into full possession of his kingdom, and secure for him the heathen as his inheritance, and the uttermost part of the earth for his possession.

It is prayer which will enable him to break his foes with a rod of iron, that will make these foes tremble in their pride and power, who are but frail potter's vessels, to be broken in pieces by one stroke of his hand. A person who can pray is the mightiest instrument Christ has in this world. A praying church is stronger than all the gates of hell.

God's decree for the glory of his Son's kingdom is dependent on prayer for its fulfillment: "Ask of me, and I will give thee the heathen for thy inheritance, and the uttermost part of the earth for thy possession." God the Father gives nothing to his Son except through prayer. And the reason why the church has not received more in the missionary work in which it is engaged is the lack of prayer. "Ye have not, because ye ask not."

Every dispensation foreshadowing the coming of Christ when the world has been evangelized, at the end of time, rests upon these constitutional provisions, God's decree, his promises, and prayer. However far away that day of victory by distance or time, or remoteness of shadowy type, prayer is the essential condition on which the dispensation becomes strong, typical, and representative. From Abraham, the first of the nation of the Israelites, the friend of God, down to this dispensation of the Holy Spirit, this has been true.

> The nations call! from sea to sea
> Extends the thrilling cry,
> Come over, Christians, if there be,
> And help us, ere we die.
>
> Our hearts, O Lord, the summons feel;
> Let hand with heart combine,
> And answer to the world's appeal,
> By giving that is thine.

Our Lord's plan for securing workers in the foreign missionary field is the same plan he set on foot for obtaining preachers. It is by the process of praying. It is the prayer plan as distinguished from all manmade plans. These mission workers are to be "sent men." God must send them. They are God-called, divinely moved to this great work. They are inwardly moved to enter the harvest fields of the world and gather sheaves for the heavenly garners. Men do not choose to be missionaries any more than they choose to be preachers. God sends out laborers in his harvest fields in answer to the prayers of his church. Here is the divine plan as set forth by our Lord:

> But when he saw the multitudes, he was moved with compassion on them, because they fainted, and were . . . as sheep having no shepherd. Then saith he unto his disciples, The harvest truly is plenteous, but the labourers are few. Pray ye there-

fore the Lord of the harvest, that he will send forth labourers
into his harvest (Matt. 9:36–38).

It is the business of the home church to do the praying. It is
the Lord's business to call and send forth the laborers. The Lord
does not do the praying. The church does not do the calling.
And just as our Lord's compassions were aroused by the sight
of multitudes, weary, hungry, and scattered, exposed to evils, as
sheep having no shepherd, so whenever the church has eyes to
see the vast multitudes of earth's inhabitants, descendants of
Adam, weary in soul, living in darkness, and wretched and sinful, will it be moved to compassion, and begin to pray the Lord
of the harvest to send forth laborers into his harvest.

Missionaries, like ministers, are born of praying people. A
praying church begets laborers in the harvest field of the world.
The scarcity of missionaries argues a non-praying church. It is
all right to send trained men to the foreign field, but first of all
they must be God-sent. The sending is the fruit of prayer. As
praying men are the occasion of sending them, so in turn the
workers must be praying men. And the prime mission of these
praying missionaries is to convert prayerless heathen men into
praying men. Prayer is the proof of their calling, their divine
credentials, and their work.

He who is not a praying man at home needs the one fitness
to become a mission worker abroad. He who has not the spirit
which moves him toward sinners at home, will hardly have a
spirit of compassion for sinners abroad. Missionaries are not
made of men who are failures at home. He who will be a man
of prayer abroad must, before anything else, be a man of prayer
in his home church. If he be not engaged in turning sinners
away from their prayerless ways at home, he will hardly succeed
in turning away the heathen from their prayerless ways. In other
words, it takes the same spiritual qualifications for being a
home worker as it does for being a foreign worker.

God in his own way, in answer to the prayers of his church,
calls men into his harvest fields. Sad will be the day when
Missionary Boards and churches overlook that fundamental fact,
and send out their own chosen men independent of God.

Is the harvest great? Are the laborers few? Then "pray ye the Lord of the harvest to send forth laborers into his harvest." Oh, that a great wave of prayer would sweep over the church asking God to send out a great army of laborers into the needy harvest fields of the earth! No danger of the Lord of the harvest sending out too many laborers and crowding the fields. He who calls will most certainly provide the means for supporting those whom he calls and sends forth.

The one great need in the modern missionary movement is intercessors. They were scarce in the days of Isaiah. This was his complaint:

> And he saw that there was no man, and wondered that there was no intercessor (Isa. 59:16).

So today there is great need of intercessors, first, for the needy harvest fields of earth, born of a Christlike compassion for the thousands without the gospel; and then intercessors for laborers to be sent forth by God into the needy fields of earth.